The
Mass
Explained

The
Mass
Explained

An Introduction to the New Roman Missal

Monsignor James P. Moroney

CATHOLIC BOOK PUBLISHING CORP.
New Jersey

IMPRIMATUR: ✠ Most Reverend Robert J. McManus
Bishop of Worcester
September 21, 2011

RESCRIPT

In accord with canon 824, of the *Code of Canon Law,* I hereby grant my permission to publish *The Mass Explained* by Rev. Msgr. James P. Moroney.

Photo credits: pp. 36, 58, and 116, Scala/Art Resource, NY; pp. 74 and 108, Erich Lessing/Art Resource, NY; p. 24, Cameraphoto Arte, Venice/Art Resource, NY.

(T-104)

ISBN 978-0-89942-104-9

Table of Contents

List of Abbreviations

BOG   *Book of the Gospels for Use in the Dioceses of the United States of America* (USCCB), Catholic Book Publishing, 2000.

BLS   *Built of Living Stones: USCCB Guidelines on Art, Architecture, and Worship*, USCCB Publications, 2000.

CCC   *Catechism of the Catholic Church* (Congregation for Doctrine of the Faith), USCCB Publications, 2000.

CE   *Ceremoniale Episcoporum* (Congregation for Divine Worship and the Discipline of the Sacraments), Libreria Editrice Vaticana, 1964.

DV   *Dei Verbum: Constitution on Divine Revelation* (Second Vatican Council).

EE   Encyclical Letter *Ecclesia de Eucharistia* (Pope John Paul II), USCCB Publications, 2003.

GIRM   *General Instruction of the Roman Missal* (USCCB), USCCB Publications, 2003.

GS   *Gaudium et Spes* (Second Vatican Council).

IOM   Introduction to the Order of Mass: A Pastoral Resource of the Committee on the Liturgy, USCCB Publications, 2002.

LFM   *Lectionary for Mass for Use in the Dioceses of the United States of America* (USCCB), Catholic Book Publishing, 2003.

LG   *Lumen Gentium* (Second Vatican Council).

MD   *Mediator Dei* (Pope Pius XI), www.vatican.va, 1947.

SC   *Sacrosanctum Concilium* (Second Vatican Council).

SCT   Apostolic Constitution *Sacramentum Caritatis* (Pope Benedict XVI), USCCB, 2007.

STL   *Sing to the Lord.*

Introduction

SOON we will have a new *Roman Missal*, although it's not really new at all. While some of the prayers and rubrics have been fine-tuned and the book reflects a bit more maturity than its predecessors on such questions as inculturation and the role of the Priest, it describes the same Mass we have been celebrating since the Lord first commanded us to "do this in memory of me."

Priests will find more accurate translations of the prayers to be a challenge, especially after having prayed from the *Sacramentary* for a half century, but even the newness of the words will soon pass. What, I pray, will not pass is the great excitement that drives the Church in her celebrations of this holy and living Sacrifice.

The People at Mass

God chose us, and God gathers us to the Cross of his Son at every Mass. Us! Of all the people in the world—the ones so much brighter than us, so much better looking than us, so much more powerful than we will ever be—he chose us "before the world began, . . . to be holy and blameless in his sight" (Eph 1:4). It was not we who chose him, but he who chose us. It is not "our Mass" which, like a town meeting or a political party we choose to form in our own image and likeness. It is his Mass, his Sacrifice to which he calls us to join our lives.

7

The Mass is for us poor little ones who have been Baptized into his paschal death and rising. For we have washed our robes in the Blood of the Lamb and have become whiter than snow (cf. Rev 7:14). Thus we have, in Holy Baptism, been consecrated as "a chosen race, a royal priesthood, a holy nation, a people claimed by God as his own" (1 Pet 2:9) to join the sacrifices of our lives to the one perfect Sacrifice of Christ upon the Cross.

In a world paralyzed by fear that too often violently rejects the gentle sacrifice of the one who opened his arms on a Cross for love of them, his disciples are often ridiculed or snidely dismissed as foolish old romantics, deluding themselves with quaint but meaningless folk tales. Sometimes, we recall the Lord's own words, "if they persecuted me, they will persecute you" (Jn 15:20).

But how wrong the world is! For God has chosen us to be his Priestly People. And this Mass is for us. It is the place to which we bring our joys and sorrows, our victories and our humiliations, our hopes and our fears. It is the source and the summit of everything that truly matters in life, our hope and our salvation, the place where we discover who we are and what we are meant to be. The Mass is for us.

The Priest at Mass

The Mass is for Priests. Over the past two decades I have been privileged to speak to more than 20,000 Priests and Deacons in more than one hundred dioceses. Priests, I have learned, are among the most wonderful of human beings. They suffer from the same pains and stresses as any other group, but they are constantly fed by a burning desire to do the right thing, to give their lives to Christ and to his Church. They are in love with their people and with the faith that Christ sends them to bring to the young and the old, the bright and the not so bright, the cheerful and the depressed, the rich and the poor, and all the people in between.

But Priests are also sometimes in sad spiritual straights. The older ones grew up in a time when the Priest was the most admired man in the community. That all changed when some of their brothers were accused of terrible crimes. Priests ordained in the decades after the Second Vatican Council sometimes feel disappointed that the utopian visions of their youth were never fully realized. Meanwhile, the younger ones often suffered under a pastoral ministry that seemed to be more intent on balloons and flowers than on faith and practice. Many of them labor under the burden of skepticism and a search for authentic authority.

Many Priests are weighed down by the bureaucracy and a media voracious for a fresh scandal. They struggle to establish meaningful priorities amidst people suffering in a world of ever-new challenges to a Christian way of life.

It's not all bad, certainly. The great majority of parishioners love their Priest more than he deserves. I will never forget the outpouring of affection upon the death of my first pastor. As their only remaining Priest, the parishioners practically anointed me with the tears they shed for this good man. The love that people hold for their parish Priest is extraordinarily durable, as recent studies on the impact of the sexual abuse scandal have shown.

But as consoling as the support of "the people" can be, it is from the Sacred Liturgy that Priest and People drink deeply of the particular charism of their respective callings and find meaning in their respective roles.

For the Catholic priest or parishioner, the Mass is the center of the day, the source and the summit of all activity, and the principal time when the Church is made manifest to them and to the world.

The Sacred Liturgy is the bridge between the daily life of the people of God and Christ, who invites them to partake of his heavenly banquet. It is the bridge between this world and the next and the Priest is the gatekeeper. In the Sacred Liturgy two great loves of the Priest's life are brought into a holy communion: the People of God and the Lord who formed them into a royal priesthood.

Our Inheritance

Thus the Mass is "left to us as an inheritance by the Lord Jesus Christ on the night before he died for us." It is the key to understanding and participating in his great saving Paschal death and Resurrection. It is the Mass, in which "the whole spiritual wealth of the Church is contained—namely Christ, our Paschal Lamb."[1]

What we call today the Eucharist, or the Liturgy, in days gone by was called simply the Lord's Supper or the Breaking of the Bread. It is the center of the whole

Christian life and we believe that all of our lives are bound up with it, flow from it, and are ordered to it.[2] Indeed, the Mass is the principal office of the Priest and the chief responsibility of each of the Baptized.

To understand such a mystery will, and this is no surprise, prove quite an undertaking. Indeed, the Church has been trying to understand "this holy and living Sacrifice" since the Lord first gathered the twelve Apostles around him in the Upper Room.

In this little book we will try, you and I, to seek this understanding in three ways. First, we will explore where the Mass came from. We will look at what the Church asks us to do at Mass. Finally, we will look at what happens at Mass and begin to explore the meaning of its words, songs, gestures and ritual actions.

In the second half of this book we will continue with an examination of the roles of the Priest, the Deacon, and the people at Mass. Finally, in the Afterword, I will offer some brief reflections on the new translation of the *Roman Missal*, the liturgical book we use for the celebration of these Sacred Rites.

All this can seem terribly complex. It is. But if we examine each of the aspects of this incredible mystery one at a time, perhaps we can grow together in our understanding of the source and the summit of the entire Christian life.

Understanding
the Mass

S. GREGORIVS

Chapter 1

Where the Mass Came From

THE Mass began in the Upper Room where Christ gathered his Apostles on that first Holy Thursday night. The earliest account of the Last Supper comes from Saint Paul's First Letter to the Corinthians:

> For what I received from the Lord I handed on to you: the Lord Jesus, on the night he was betrayed, took bread, and after giving thanks he broke it and said, "This is my body that is for you. Do this in remembrance of me."
>
> In the same fashion, after the supper, he also took the cup and said, "This cup is the new covenant in my blood. Whenever you drink it, do this in remembrance of me." And so, whenever you eat this bread and drink the cup, you proclaim the death of the Lord until he comes (11:23-26).

Every Mass celebrated since the Last Supper has followed this same basic structure:

- Just as Jesus spoke with his disciples, so all gather in church and the Priest calls them to join their hearts and minds with Christ. Then Christ speaks to us in the Liturgy of the Word, whose high point is the proclamation of the Gospel.

- Just as Jesus took bread, so at the beginning of the Liturgy of the Eucharist the people bring forth gifts of bread and wine which are placed upon the altar by the Priest.

- Just as Jesus gave thanks, so the Priest prays the great Eucharistic Prayer over the gifts of bread and wine, and God transforms them into the Body and Blood of his only-begotten Son.

- Just as Jesus broke the bread, so the Liturgy of the Eucharist comes to completion with the Breaking of the Bread and the distribution of Holy Communion to all the gathered faithful.

By the beginning of the second century, the Mass had begun to take shape, as we see from a letter written by Saint Justin to the Emperor Antoninus Pius:

On the day named after the sun, all who live in city or countryside assemble in the same place. The memoirs of the apostles or the writings of the prophets are read for as long as time allows. When the lector has finished, the president addresses us and exhorts us to imitate the splendid things we have heard. Then we all stand and pray. As we have said earlier, when we have finished praying, bread, wine, and water are brought up. The president then prays and gives thanks according to his ability. And the people give their assent with *Amen!* Next, the gifts which have been *eucharistified* are distributed, and everyone shares in them, while they are also sent via the deacons to the absent brethren.[1]

From the first days of the Church, then, we can see a Mass beginning to emerge which is very similar to the one we celebrate today. Of course there are major differences between today and the earliest centuries. During the period of Christian persecutions it was illegal to meet in large assembly halls or churches, so Christians met in "house churches" belonging to their wealthier members.

This "age of the martyrs" witnessed extraordinary heroism by those who gave their lives for the faith. They were sustained in their heroic witness by the Holy Eucharist, as exemplified by Saint Ignatius of Antioch when he wrote shortly before he was thrown to the lions for refusing to deny the Lord Jesus:

> I want the bread of God, which is the flesh of Jesus Christ . . . and for drink I want his blood, the sign of his imperishable love . . . I am his wheat and I shall be ground by the teeth of beasts that I may become Christ's pure bread.

Saint Ignatius and other commentators bear witness to the fact that Bishops and Priests were the presiders at these "house church Masses" and also provide evidence that lay liturgical ministries were beginning to evolve. The Mass in this age lacked the solemn ceremonial that larger gatherings would foster in later years, but the witness of those giving their lives for the faith must have lent an eloquence and a beauty to these more intimate domestic celebrations.

With the legalization of Christianity by the Emperor Constantine in 313 A.D., Christianity emerged as a pub-

lic religion, whose Liturgy was celebrated in grandiose
Roman basilicas. These rectangular buildings with rows
of columns and a semicircular apse at one end still
provide the pattern for many Catholic churches of the
twenty-first century.

While even in these massive basilicas the basic
structure of the Mass was to remain the same, this
more solemn and formal setting definitely had its
effect. Processions with ranks of ornately vested ministers were accompanied by chants, candles, and
incense. Gone was the earnest intimacy of a persecuted few meeting in the occasional house. In its place was
the Church Triumphant celebrating with every resource
imaginable.

This shift from the intimate to the solemn is reflected
even in the prayers that were prayed at Mass. The
Didache is an early collection of Mass texts from the time
of the house churches, and it describes a part of the
Eucharistic Prayer that prays for the needs of the
Church:

> Lord, remember your Church
> and deliver it from all evil;
> make it perfect in your love
> and gather it from the four winds,
> this sanctified Church,
> into the kingdom you have prepared for it,
> for power and glory are yours through all ages![2]

Compare this simple prayer to what is today the
Roman Canon (Eucharistic Prayer I), which would have

first been heard in one of those enormous basilica Masses of the fifth century:

> ... for your holy catholic Church.
> Be pleased to grant her peace,
> to guard, unite and govern her
> throughout the whole world,
> together with your servant N.
> our Pope and N. our Bishop,
> and all Bishops who,
> holding to the truth,
> hand on the catholic and apostolic faith.

With this new formality came a need to approve prayers and to collect them into books of prayers *(Sacramentaries)* and readings from the Bible *(Lectionaries)*. In addition, ministries of liturgical service were formalized and established by the Bishop,

The clarification of doctrinal disputes by Popes and Councils were not without their effect on the Liturgy. Great preachers, such as Saint Augustine (Bishop of Hippo in northern Africa) and Saint Ambrose (Bishop of Milan in northern Italy) fought against a wide range of heresies concerning the divinity of Christ (Arianism), our need for God to save us (Pelagianism), and the rebaptism of reconciled heretics (Donatism). The writings of these "Fathers of the Church" also greatly influenced the prayers and preaching of the emerging Liturgy.

As the Church began to spread across Europe, new architectural forms and new types of ceremonial changed the Mass in many ways. The gothic cathedral, with its soaring arches and walls of light, wondrously expressed the beauty and transcendence of God, though sometimes at the risk of distancing the people from the liturgical action. The richness of Gallican ritual forms introduced a blazing fire on Easter eve, while a growing preoccupation with the need to beg God's mercy infused the prayers and rites of the Mass.

The distancing of the Liturgy from the ordinary Christian in this period is of great significance. Latin, the language of the Mass prayers, was no longer popularly understood. Lay liturgical ministries, including liturgical choirs, were now made up exclusively of clerics. Even the reception of Holy Communion was less frequent, resulting in the need for the Fourth Lateran Council in 1215 to remind Catholics that they should receive Holy Communion at least once a year.

With time, the Mass emerged as something the people came to see, not as a sacred work in which they took an active part. One contributing factor was the denial by some that Jesus was truly present under the forms of Bread and Wine consecrated at Mass. In reaction, the Blessed Sacrament became more and more an object to be adored and not the Bread of Life to be eaten at every Mass.

While Martin Luther and other Protestant reformers set out to address some of these issues in the early sixteenth century, their overly zealous and sometimes overly simplified solutions resulted in divisions in the Christian family that continue to this day. The Bishops of the Council of Trent made significant strides in responding to many of these challenges by reforming the Liturgy and consolidating the diverse celebrations of the Mass into a single *Roman Missal.*

The Fathers of the Council of Trent were, however, faced with assaults on the Church from every side. On the one hand, Liturgy was rooted in superstitions and secondary elements were widespread. The liturgical rites and texts varied greatly from region to region, thus threatening the very identity of the Roman Rite. On the other hand, the wholesale rejection of key doctrinal teachings by the reformers threatened the authentic handing on of the Catholic faith.

The pronouncements of the Council of Trent resulted in decrees and an entirely new *Roman Missal,* which sought to insure unity and consistency of belief in revealed Catholic truth, while at the same time exhibiting a remarkable pastoral sensitivity.

The Tridentine Fathers insisted that even when Liturgy was to be celebrated in Latin, it should be frequently explained to the faithful. Similarly, a renewed premium was placed on the internal participation of the faithful in the Liturgy, requiring that the Mass be celebrated "with interior cleanliness and purity of heart, and with a piety that finds outward expression."[3]

By the late nineteenth century, an increasing popular and scholarly interest in the texts and rites of the Roman Liturgy led to a liturgical movement, embraced by several Popes and culminating in the convening of the Second

Vatican Council by Pope John XXIII in 1960. The first document of that Council sought to continue the work of the Council of Trent and called for a new reform of the Sacred Liturgy. Issued in 1963, *Sacrosanctum Concilium* mandated reforms of the *Roman Missal* and the other liturgical books in the interest of the full, conscious, and active participation of the faithful in the Liturgy, a goal that the Council Fathers mandated be considered "before all else." The Council Fathers mandated that among the many considerations in reforming the Mass, special attention should be given to assuring that:

the revised rites express more clearly the holy things they signify;[4]

the treasures of the bible be made more widely available;[5]

in all this, the full, conscious, and active participation of the people be considered before all else.[6]

These reforms, and others, were accomplished over a period of several years following the close of the Second Vatican Council and resulted in the Mass we celebrate today. Upon their promulgation, Pope Paul VI expressed his confident hope "that the faithful will receive the new Missal as a help toward witnessing and strengthening their unity with one another; that through the new Missal one and the same prayer in great diversity of languages will ascend, more fragrant than any incense, to our heavenly Father, through our High Priest Jesus Christ, in the Holy Spirit."[7]

In 2000, Pope John Paul II promulgated the third post-conciliar edition of the *Roman Missal,* a work whose translation in English was completed in 2011.

FOR DISCUSSION

1. The biblical accounts of the Last Supper use the verbs took, blessed, broke, gave. Discuss how these apply to the Mass as celebrated in your parish today.

2. What might the Mass have meant to Christians in the time of the persecutions in the early Church? Discuss what life must have been personally for those whose friends and relatives were martyred and how this might have affected how they celebrated the Mass.

3. How were the "house church" Masses different from the Masses celebrated in basilicas?

4. How did participation in the Mass differ in different ages of the Church?

5. Name three reforms of the Mass intended by the Fathers of the Second Vatican Council and explain how they have affected the way we celebrate the Liturgy.

6. Name a reform of the Mass intended by the Fathers of the Second Vatican Council and explain how it has not yet been fully realized.

Chapter 2

What We Do at Mass

THE Mass celebrates heavenly realities and spiritual truth, but it does so by "signs perceptible to the senses."[1] While, therefore, the prayers of our hearts and the thoughts of our minds are essential, we must constantly strive to conform them to what we see and hear and smell and touch at Mass. It is through these concrete signs that we join ourselves to Christ, who took on human flesh that we might know heavenly realities.

Posture

We have already seen how postures in the Mass are assumed by the entire liturgical assembly and both express and reinforce our unity and our dedication to being One Body in Christ. But how does a common posture help each one of us to pray?

We pray at Mass through our bodies, just as we do with our voices, our minds, and our hearts. And each of the postures we assume at Mass means something and tells us about the action in which we are taking a part.

When we stand, we show respect, and are reminded that we have risen with Jesus to the dignity of the children of God. So we stand for the Entrance Procession, the Opening Rites, the Gospel, going up to receive Holy Communion, and for the closing prayer.

When we kneel we are reminded of our sinfulness, but most of all of how we are so little and God is so big! This is why we usually kneel in private prayer and for the Eucharistic Prayer at Mass.

When we sit we are naturally disposed to listen and to meditate on the meaning of the words we hear. Thus sitting is an ideal posture for listening to the readings and the Homily.

Even the postures we assume make us one with Christ, who died for us upon the Cross and who rose to give eternal life to these lowly bodies of ours.

Genuflections and Bows

Speaking of postures, we might here say a word about genuflections and bows.

We genuflect by bending the right knee to the ground. Genuflection is used to express adoration of God. This is why we genuflect before the Blessed Sacrament when we enter the church, or whenever, outside of Mass, we pass in front of the tabernacle. We also genuflect to the Holy Cross on Good Friday.

We bow to show reverence and honor. We bow our heads at the naming of the persons of the Blessed Trinity, the names of Jesus, of his Blessed Mother, and the Saint of the day. We bow our bodies (from the waist) at the words in the Nicene Creed which remind us of the mystery of the incarnation of the Lord.[2]

The Priest and the other ministers genuflect and bow at many other times prescribed by their roles and duties.

Song

Singing is an essential part of the Mass because it so naturally leads us beyond ourselves and so clearly expresses the communal nature of the Liturgy. The Bishops of the United States have published a guide to singing in Church called *Sing to the Lord,* in which they have this to say:

> Music is . . . a sign of God's love for us and of our love for him. In this sense, it is very personal. But unless music sounds, it is not music, and whenever it sounds, it is accessible to others. By its very nature song has both an individual and a communal dimension. Thus, it is no wonder that singing together in church expresses so well the sacramental presence of God to his people.[3]

After the Last Supper, the Lord sang a hymn with his Apostles on the way to his Blessed Passion, and the use of hymns, canticles, and psalms has been a part of the Mass ever since. When we sing at Mass, our voices are always blended with the angels and saints of the great heavenly choir, who are "holding their harps given them by God and singing the song of Moses, the servant of God, and the song of the Lamb" (cf. Rev 15:3).

This is why the Bishops of the United States remind us that at the Mass:

> Participation must . . . be external, so that internal participation can be expressed and reinforced by actions, gestures, and bodily attitudes, and by the acclamations, responses, and singing. The quality of our participation in such sung praise comes less from our vocal ability than from the desire of our hearts to sing together of our love for God.

Participation in the Sacred Liturgy both expresses and strengthens the faith that is in us.[4]

Silence

Silence sometimes says more than words. We live amidst a cacophony of noises, broadcasts, and accompanying tunes. Silence somehow washes that all away and invites us to a place deep within, a sanctuary where God comes to meet us.

The Liturgy uses silence to foster disposition, meditation, and recollection. Even before the Mass begins, we are called on to be silent in order to dispose ourselves to the awesome mysteries we are about to celebrate. After each of the readings and the homily, we meditate on the meaning of what we have heard so that it might sink in to our minds and our hearts. After receiving Holy Communion we sit in silence, recalling the Lord who has given himself to us as food and who now lives in us as we live in him.

There is no word as powerful as silence. Silence cannot be done in haste. Only silence can enable us to embrace with our hearts what is being prayed, sung, or said. Silence must come before action, and the only reaction worthy to follow a meeting with God is kneeling in silence, humility, and joy.

Pope Benedict XVI has recommended Saint Joseph as an example for each of us who seeks to cultivate an interior quiet.

[Saint Joseph's] silence is steeped in contemplation of the mystery of God in an attitude of total availability to the divine desires. In other words,

Saint Joseph's silence does not express an inner emptiness but, on the contrary, the fullness of the faith he bears in his heart and which guides his every thought and action.

It is a silence thanks to which Joseph, in unison with Mary, watches over the Word of God, known through the Sacred Scriptures, continuously comparing it with the events of the life of Jesus; a silence woven of constant prayer, a prayer of blessing of the Lord, of the adoration of his holy will, and of unreserved entrustment to his providence. . . . Let us allow ourselves to be "filled" with Saint Joseph's silence! In a world that is often too noisy, that encourages neither recollection nor listening to God's voice, we are in such deep need of it. During this season of preparation for Christmas, let us cultivate inner recollection in order to welcome and cherish Jesus in our own lives.[5]

Reverence

The liturgical reform in the first years of the twenty-first century has experienced a deep and growing desire for reverence in the Liturgy. In 2006, Cardinal Francis Arinze addressed the question, suggesting that nothing is more important than reverence.

Indeed, we can say that the most important thing in divine worship is not that we understand every word or concept. No. The most important consideration is that we stand in reverence and awe before God, that we adore, praise and thank him. The sacred, the things of God, are best approached with sandals off.[6]

When Moses approached God on Mount Sinai, he took off his shoes. Like Moses, when we approach the all-holy, the all-powerful God in the Sacred Liturgy, our only possible reaction is reverence, adoration, and bowing ourselves very low.

We bow very low when we approach the altar. We also show reverence for the altar by kissing it, and clothing it with cloths or candles. We reverence the Priest with a greeting that recognizes the role God has given him, and most of all we, with a genuflection, reverence Christ Jesus in the Blessed Sacrament reserved in the tabernacle.

We also reverence God's people with The Rite of Peace. Indeed, we are called to express our belief that Christ has gathered us into a Royal Priesthood by our deep sense of reverence for God and charity toward our brothers and sisters who celebrate the Mass with us.[7]

We show reverence at Mass with our hearts, when, during the Eucharistic Prayer, we observe a silence which characterizes true reverence.[8] The ways in which this reverence and charity are expressed is described by the *Roman Missal*:

> Thus, they are to avoid any appearance of singularity or division, keeping in mind that they have only one Father in heaven and that hence are all brothers or sisters to each other. Moreover, they are to form one body, whether in hearing the Word of God, or in taking part in the prayers and the

singing, or above all by the common offering of Sacrifice and by participating at the Lord's table. This unity is beautifully apparent from the gestures and postures observed together by the faithful. The faithful, moreover, should not refuse to serve the People of God gladly whenever they are asked to perform some particular service or function in the celebration.[9]

In an address to a body of liturgists in 1999, Archbishop Jerome Hanus, OSB, then chairman of the USCCB Committee on the Liturgy, reflected on this need for reverence:

> Shunning individualism, fostering unity, seeking not so much to express myself as to express the one Lord through whom we live one faith in one Baptism. This is true reverence: to die to myself and my needs and to live according to the will of Christ and his body, the Church.[10]

Preparation

So we come together in church and spend some time in prayer to prepare ourselves to celebrate these sacred mysteries. As soon as we arrive in church there are certain traditional Catholic practices that help us to prepare ourselves.

We make the Sign of the Cross with Holy Water to remind us of our Baptism. For it is through Baptism that we have become one with Christ and can celebrate these sacred mysteries. A non-baptized friend could certainly attend our Mass. But only one who has been baptized in

Christ has become a part of Christ's Royal Priesthood and can celebrate this holy and living sacrifice.

We genuflect before the tabernacle, for we believe that Christ is truly present in the consecrated hosts it contains. Once they were little wafers of bread. Through the power of the Holy Mass they have been transformed into the very Body of Christ.

We bow to the altar, for here the Sacrifice will be offered and from here we will take part in the Holy Banquet.

Then we kneel or sit and pray, perhaps using the words of the Psalmist: "my heart is ready O God, my heart is ready!" Or, perhaps, we will pray one of the other great prayers written by the saints to prepare themselves for the celebration of Mass.

PRAYER[11]

Almighty eternal God,
behold, I come to the Sacrament
of your Only Begotten Son,
our Lord Jesus Christ,
as one sick to the physician of life,
as one unclean to the fountain of mercy,
as one blind to the light of eternal brightness,
as one poor and needy to the Lord of heaven and
    earth.
I ask, therefore, for the abundance of your immense
    generosity,
that you may graciously cure my sickness,

wash away my defilement,
give light to my blindness,
enrich my poverty,
clothe my nakedness,
so that I may receive the bread of Angels,
the King of kings and Lord of lords,
with such reverence and humility,
such contrition and devotion,
such purity and faith,
such purpose and intention
as are conducive to the salvation of my soul.
Grant, I pray, that I may receive
not only the Sacrament of the Lord's Body and Blood,
but also the reality and power of that Sacrament.
O most gentle God,
grant that I may so receive
the Body of your Only Begotten Son our Lord Jesus
    Christ,
which he took from the Virgin Mary,
that I may be made worthy to be incorporated into his
    Mystical Body
and to be counted among its members.
O most loving Father,
grant that I may at last gaze for ever
upon the unveiled face of your beloved Son
whom I, a wayfarer,
propose to receive now veiled under these species:
Who lives and reigns with you for ever and ever.
Amen.

FOR DISCUSSION

1. Give examples of when Catholics genuflect or bow.

2. Why is silence important at Mass?

3. Discuss what it means to be reverent at Mass.

4. Why is song important to the Sacred Liturgy?

5. Discuss how we should prepare for Mass, both before we get to church and once we get there.

Understanding
What We Celebrate

Chapter 3

Understanding the Introductory Rites

HOW we begin the Mass says a lot about who we are and why we are gathered.

Why do we go to church? Is it out of habit or a family tradition? Is it because I have finally figured out that I need church? Is it because I was "born a Catholic"?

We go to church not of our own initiative, but because we have been invited. Christ Jesus, who gave his life for me, invited me at the Last Supper when he said to his Apostles and to us: "Do this in memory of me." So when I go to Mass it was never my idea in the first place. My participation in Sunday Mass is nothing more than a response from Jesus to his disciples to gather on "The day of the resurrection . . . the day of Christians . . . our day. . . . "[1]

The Introductory Rites of the Mass, then, have two purposes: to form us into one people in Christ and to dispose our hearts to receive what God is about to give us in word and sacrament.

Christ gathers all the children of the Church to himself and to his perfect sacrifice of praise.

We know that Christ is present in this holy assembly, for he has assured us that where two or three are gathered in his name, there he is in the midst of them (cf. Mt 18:20). Christ is also present in the Priest presiding in his person, in his word proclaimed, and, in a continuing way, in the Blessed Sacrament.[2]

We Begin with a Procession

After everyone has arrived, the Priest, accompanied by the Deacon and the other ministers, processes through the gathered assembly and goes to the altar.

The procession is not just a way of getting the main players to their places! It is designed to help us to be aware that Christ has formed us into a Holy Priesthood. This is why the Priest and the ministers pass through the gathered faithful and why we sing with one voice the Entrance Chant or Song. The Entrance Procession and its Song are both designed to weave us together so that we can recognize ourselves as one people, One Body in Christ.

The procession is usually led by the Cross, accompanied by ministers with lighted candles, and sometimes by burning incense. Altar servers, lectors, and other liturgical ministers follow. At the end of the procession is the Deacon, followed by the Priest.

For the entire rest of the Liturgy, each of these ministers will perform a particular role in the Sacred Liturgy. The Priest will act in the person of Christ, gathering up our prayers and offering them to the Father. The Deacon will serve as an intermediary, bringing the Gospel to us, and assisting us in bringing our gifts to God. The lector will proclaim the sacred scriptures, the cantor and psalmist will help us to sing, and the ushers will keep good order. The altar servers will assist with the practicalities around the altar, and other ministers will perform particular services according to their assigned tasks.

Greeting of the Altar and of the People Gathered Together

When they arrive in the sanctuary, all greet the altar with a bow, while the clergy kiss the altar. The altar is a primary sign of the presence of Christ, who is the altar and the sacrifice, the giver and the gift. Once a lifeless stone, this altar is now the stone of life upon which lifeless bread is placed to become the bread of life.[3] Thus we begin by bowing to Christ and kissing him in a sign of affection, veneration, and greeting.

On more solemn occasions the Priest may incense the altar and the Cross. Incense is made up of a granulated form of aromatic resins and spices. When placed on burning pieces of charcoal in a censer (also known as a thurible) the incense turns into a sweet-smelling white smoke. Incense was burned morning and night in the Temple in Jerusalem and is frequently mentioned by the prophets. Thus do we hear that the Jewish Priest Zechariah was burning incense when he received the promise that a son would be born to him (cf. Lk 1:8-11). So do our prayers rise like incense before God's heavenly throne (cf. Ps 141:2, Rev 8:3-4).

The Chair

Then the Priest goes to his chair. This is no ordinary chair. Just as the Bishop's chair (called a *cathedra*) in the cathedral is reserved only for him, so the Priest's chair in the parish is reserved only for the one who, in the place of the Bishop, is the chief shepherd, teacher, and sanctifi-er of the community.[4]

The Sign of the Cross

Once the Priest has reached his chair, he leads every-one in doing the same thing every Catholic does at the beginning of every prayer: he makes the Sign of the Cross. In the Sign of the Cross we profess our faith in the Blessed Trinity and in our crucified Savior.

The Priest says: **In the name of the Father, and of the Son, and of the Holy Spirit.**

The people reply: **Amen.**

In the earliest days of the Church, the Sign of the Cross was made on the forehead, in the same way a child is signed by his parents and godparents in Baptism today. This sealing *(sphragis)* with the cross was a statement that this person now belongs to Christ and to his Cross.

We make this Sign of the Cross over our whole being, from forehead to chest, and from arm to arm, for our whole being belongs to Christ and to his Cross. This is the sign of our redemption, the sign of victory, and the sign of glory.

It is through the Cross that we enter into the life of the Most Blessed Trinity. So we claim the love between the Father and Son in the unity of the Holy Spirit as our new home. Through the Cross of Jesus we are inserted into that life and not only pray but live and move and have our being in the name of the Father, and of the Son, and of the Holy Spirit.

The great liturgical pioneer of the first half of the last century, Fr. Romano Guardini, once wrote of this Sign of the Cross:

> When we cross ourselves, let it be with a real Sign of the Cross. Instead of a small, cramped gesture that gives no notion of its meaning, let us make a large, unhurried sign, from forehead to breast, from shoulder to shoulder, consciously feeling how it includes the whole of us, our thoughts, our attitudes, our body and soul, every part of us all at once, how it consecrates and sanctifies us. . . . [5]

Greeting

Having been gathered by Christ into the life of the Most Blessed Trinity, we are then greeted by the Priest, who, acting in the person of Christ *(in persona Christi)* extends his hands in a gesture of greeting to everyone present:

The Priest says: **The Lord be with you** (cf. Rom 2:4).

The people reply: **And with your spirit.**

The Lord be with you.

This greeting is really a prayer, whose origins lie in the Old Testament, such as when Ruth would go out to glean what was left of the corn. The owners of the field would greet the poor gleaners with "The Lord be with you," and they would respond to the generous farmers "The Lord bless you!" (cf. Ru 2:4).

The greeting is not unlike the greeting of the angel to the Blessed Virgin at the Annunciation, "Hail, full of grace, the Lord is with you"(cf. Lk 1:28). Just as the Lord dwelled within the womb of the Mother of the Church, so the Christ, Emmanuel (cf. Mt 1:23), will remain with us always until the end of time.

Finally, we might reflect on the ironic kinship of the greeting "The Lord be with you," with the way we bid farewell to one other in everyday speech. The English language salutation "good-bye" was originally "God be with you,"a prayer not unlike the greeting at Mass, whose profundity is all but totally obscured by its common use.[6]

And with your spirit.

But just as this is no ordinary greeting, there is no ordinary response. The greeting achieves a level of intimacy as the one who has been ordained to act in the person of Christ prays the first prayer of the Mass for the sheep he has been called to shepherd.

This holy people then respond to the Priest concluding the most ancient dialogue of the Sacred Liturgy. It is a response which dates to the Apostolic Tradition in the West (circa 215 A.D.) and at least to the time of Saint John Chrysostom in the East.

The response recognizes the unique reality of the one who has been anointed to act in the person of Christ by addressing the spirit he has received in sacred ordination. It is the spirit referenced in the ancient prayer by which he was ordained. Like the spirit which God sent down upon the seventy wise men to help Moses to rule the Israelites, like the spirit which God sent upon the sons of Aaron that they might offer sacrifice in the

Temple, this spirit is given to every Priest at his ordination that he might offer the sacrifice of Christ in union with the faithful and for their nourishment.

This dialogue will be repeated by Priest and people each time the Priest is about to pray or bless or proclaim on their behalf. It is, to use a contemporary phrase, a statement of right relationships, a dialogue between a shepherd and his flock, between Christ and his Priestly People, between the one ordained to act in the person of Christ and the Holy People for and with whom he will offer this holy and living sacrifice.

Two Other Greetings

Two other greetings may be used by the Priest at this time. One is taken from the final verse of the Second Letter of Saint Paul to the Corinthians (13:13). Like the Sign of the Cross, it invokes the Blessed Trinity:

The Priest: **The grace of our Lord Jesus Christ,**
and the love of God,
and the communion of the Holy Spirit
be with you all.

The people reply: **And with your spirit.**

Here Saint Paul asks that the unity of the most Blessed Trinity, the source of all unity, be the source of unity in the life of the Church. Just as the Father loves the Son with a paternal, creative love, and the Son loves the Father with an obedient, filial love, and their life is defined by this life, by the (communion of the Holy Spirit), so the Priest asks that the Church be so deeply inserted into the life of the Most Blessed Trinity that they might be one as God is one (cf. Jn 17:21).

The third formula is frequently used by Saint Paul to begin his epistles (cf. Eph 1:2; Gal 1:3):

> The Priest: **Grace to you and peace**
> **from God our Father**
> **and the Lord Jesus Christ.**

The people reply: **And with your spirit.**

Having greeted Christ in the altar and the people gathered in the Lord's name, the Priest[7] then briefly introduces the Mass of the day and then invites all present to acknowledge their sins in an Act of Penitence.

The Act of Penitence

Most meetings begin the same way. The participants each pronounce a polite greeting, maybe exchange some words, and then sit down to the first order of business: getting to know each other. "I'm Sarah Smith, the organist." "Nice to meet you Sarah, do you know Michael, he's a psychologist and Mary-Anne, our parish nurse." "And I'm Father Smith, the pastor. . . . "

As you read this, similar meetings are going on all across town: at the bank, the school, and the grocery store. And each one begins the same way: by figuring out who we are.

Like these civic assemblies, the Mass is a gathering of like-minded people. They greet one another, and in a formal and deeper way, as we have seen, the Priest exchanges a greeting with them in the name of Christ. But there is a difference between the liturgical assembly and all other assemblies.

Unlike a civic assembly, which always begins by centering on its credentials, the liturgical assembly centers on God, from its first to its final moments. It's not who Monsignor Moroney is that matters. It's who Christ is, present to his mystical Body in this, his chosen Priest.

This is even more true of the Act of Penitence, which begins with the Priest asking us to quietly call to mind our sins. What matters in this assembly, gathered for the worship of God, is not all that we've accomplished, but that we are sinners and that Christ died to save us.

For while the Church is pure and innocent (Eph 5:27), we, her children, are like the prodigal son, too often concerned with selfishness and sin. Indeed, as Father Lucien Deiss has said so well: The holiness of the Church "consists precisely in recognizing herself a sinner in order to be able to welcome the forgiveness of Jesus."[8]

The First Form

This is especially true of the first form of the Act of Penitence: the Act of Contrition.

All pray:

I confess to almighty God,
and to you, my brothers and sisters,
that I have greatly sinned,
in my thoughts and in my words,
in what I have done
and in what I have failed to do,

and, striking their breast, they say:

**through my fault, through my fault,
through my most grievous fault;**

then they continue:

**therefore I ask blessed Mary ever-Virgin,
all the angels and saints,
and you, my brothers and sisters,
to pray for me to the Lord our God.**

This prayer is divided into two parts. In the first part I confess that I have sinned grievously by acts and omissions through my own fault. That's quite a way to introduce yourself to God and to the people standing next to you: I have sinned. Pray for me! I am the Prodigal who has run home to the Father to say, I have sinned!

The second part of the Act of Contrition asks the angels and the saints and everyone present "to pray for me to the Lord, our God." And here is the heart of the Act of Penitence: it is not just a reporting of what a wretch I am: it is a proclamation of the power of God to forgive my sins. It is the assurance that the Father will run out to meet me, embrace me, and welcome me home each time I turn from sin and remember the Gospel!

The same is true of the two other forms of general confession: they confess not just our sins, but Christ's willingness and power to forgive us!

The Second Form

The second form of the Act of Penitence uses verses from the penitential Psalms (cf. Ps 85:8):

℣. **Have mercy on us, O Lord.**

℟. **For we have sinned against you.**

℣. **Show us, O Lord, your mercy.**

℟. **And grant us your salvation.**

The Third Form

The third form consists of acclamations extolling Christ's merciful power, to which we respond: *Lord, have mercy* and *Christ, have mercy,* alternately.

The Priest says: **You were sent to heal the contrite of heart: Lord, have mercy**.

All respond: **Lord, have mercy.**

The Priest says: **You came to call sinners: Christ, have mercy.**

All respond: **Christ, have mercy.**

The Priest says: **You are seated at the right hand of the Father to intercede for us: Lord, have mercy.**

All respond: **Lord, have mercy.**

Each of the three forms of the Act of Penitence begins the same way, with an invitation by the Priest to quietly recall our need for God's abundant mercy. This is followed by one of three formulas of general confession and is concluded by the Priest's Prayer of Absolution.

The Prayer of Absolution

In the Prayer of Absolution, the Priest asks Almighty God to forgive our sins and lead us to everlasting life.

The Priest says: **May Almighty God have mercy on us,**
forgive us our sins,
and bring us to everlasting life.

All respond: **Amen.**

It is important to understand that this Prayer of Absolution does not take the place of the need to confess our sins. Only the Absolution we receive in the Sacrament of Penance takes away our sins definitively.

Kyrie Eleison! Christe Eleison!

The Kyrie is always a part of the Act of Penitence, whether included in its chants or sung at its conclusion. This is because the ancient Greek chant *Kyrie Eleison* (Lord, have mercy), *Christe Eleison* (Christ, have mercy) is one of the oldest and most treasured prayers of the Catholic Church.

The Kyrie is also the only prayer of the Mass in the original language of the Gospels: Greek! It is, therefore, the prayer of the two blind men begging to see (Mt 9:29), of Bartimaeus (Mk 10:47-48), and of the Canaanite woman for her little daughter (Mt 15:22). As Father Lucien Deiss once wrote so beautifully:

> The litany of the Kyrie is the liturgy of human misery, imploring the mercy of Jesus on Galilean roads. Can it not remain the litany of our misery on the road of our life?[9]

Most of the time, then, the Mass begins by recalling our sins and God's mercy. It has been that way since just a few decades after the Church was born, when the *Didache* reports (in our earliest description of the Mass) that all assemble on Sundays for the breaking of the bread "after having confessed their sins." Perhaps the Church is cognizant of her need to fulfill the Lord's command to go and be reconciled with your brother before coming to offer your sacrifice (Mt 5:23-25). Or perhaps we just realize how blessed we are to have a God who is so rich in mercy!

Sunday Blessing and Sprinkling of Holy Water

Sometimes at Sunday Mass, Holy Water is blessed and sprinkled on the people as a reminder of their Baptism. This rite begins as the Priest invites all to recall their Baptism in Christ and pray that God will bless the water that is held before him and keep us faithful to the Spirit Christ has given us. Then the Priest extends his hands over the water:

The Priest prays: **Almighty ever-living God,**
who willed that through water,
the fountain of life and the source of purification,
even souls should be cleansed
and receive the gift of eternal life;
be pleased, we pray, to ✠ bless this water,
by which we seek protection on this your day, O Lord.
Renew the living spring of your grace within us,

> **and grant that by this water we may**
> **be defended**
> **from all ills of spirit and body,**
> **and so approach you with hearts**
> **made clean**
> **and worthily receive your salvation.**
> **Through Christ our Lord.**

All respond: **Amen.**

Then, as a baptismal song is sung, the Priest sprinkles all the baptized with the water. When he returns to his place he prays a prayer similar to the Prayer of Absolution at the end of the Act of Penitence:

The Priest prays: **May almighty God cleanse us of our**
> **sins,**
> **and through the celebration of this**
> **Eucharist**
> **make us worthy to share at the table**
> **of his Kingdom.**

All respond: **Amen.**

Other Rites

At other times the Church celebrates other Introductory Rites, including the processions of Passion Sunday and the Feast of the Presentation of the Lord, the greeting of the body in the Order of Christian Funerals, or the solemn lighting of the new fire at the Easter Vigil.

The Gloria

The Gloria, which is also called the Greater Doxology or the Angelic Hymn, is a kind of non-biblical Psalm, a venerable hymn which in its earliest form was used at morning prayer but soon came to be sung at the Pope's Christmas Mass and is today used at more solemn Masses throughout the Church year.

All sing: **Glory to God in the highest,**
and on earth peace to people of good will.
We praise you, we bless you, we adore you,
we glorify you, we give you thanks for your
great glory,
Lord God, heavenly King,
O God, almighty Father.
Lord Jesus Christ, Only Begotten Son,
Lord God, Lamb of God, Son of the Father,
you take away the sins of the world,
have mercy on us;
you take away the sins of the world,
receive our prayer;
you are seated at the right hand of the
Father,
have mercy on us.
For you alone are the Holy one,
you alone are the Lord,
you alone are the most High, Jesus Christ,
with the Holy Spirit,
in the glory of God the Father. Amen.

The Gloria begins with the song of the angels announcing the birth of Christ *(Glory to God in the highest, and on earth peace to people of good will,* cf. Lk 2:14) and then opens up a hymn of praise to God the Father, and Christ the Lamb of God.

In the opening words of the Gloria we ask for two things: Glory to God and peace for us. Just as his glory extends to the farthest reaches of the heavens and then comes to dwell on earth in the incarnate Son of God, so does our praise rise up to God "in the highest" and echo among all the people of God here below. The song then bluntly states its purpose: to praise, bless, adore, glorify, and thank God for his great glory. In reflecting on this line more than seventy years ago, Father Paul Bussard wrote:

> Why should we thank God because God's glory is great? One must really love God to do so. We thank God not only because he has revealed his glory and made us sharers in it, but rather because God is so great, so beautiful, so magnificent. To know that is our happiness, our holiness. We thank him because he is sufficient in himself and of himself, because he has no need of any creature to contribute to his happiness. We rejoice, we thank him, because he is what he is.[10]

The next two lines are addressed to God the Father, our heavenly and almighty King. All this, and the hymn is only halfway done!

The rest of the hymn is addressed to Christ, the Lamb of God. There is a wonderful parallel here between this hymn at the beginning of the Liturgy and the Lamb of God that we will sing just before receiving Holy Communion. We begin, end, and celebrate the whole Mass with constant reminders that what we are about is the mercy of God!

The whole Mass, then, like the heavenly banquet at the end of time that will be our heaven, is one grand chorus of joyous praise of those who washed their robes in the Blood of the Lamb gathered around his throne. To understand the Lamb of God is to understand the Mass and to understand the meaning of life.

Our lives and our participation in the Mass are but a response to the Baptist's call, "Behold the Lamb of God, behold him who takes away the sins of the world" This is the same Lamb who was slain for our sins and by whose Precious Blood we have been redeemed. This is the Lamb who will reign forever in the Kingdom of Heaven, our light and our life, and who shall praise eternally with all the just, "Worthy is the Lamb to receive power and glory and honor. . . ."

The Collect (Opening Prayer)

In the first days of the Church, the Mass was a lot simpler than it is today. Saint Augustine tells us that in the fourth century he would come into the church, greet the people, and say the Collect Prayer. The hinges of the Introductory Rites, then, are the Greeting and the Collect.

The Collect does what its name describes: it collects the prayers of all who are gathered. Then the Priest gathers them into one and prays to God, using prayers that are often among the most ancient and theologically rich in the Treasury of the Church.

The Collect begins when the Priest invites the people: *Let us pray.* This is followed by a period of silence, during which we each offer the intentions dearest to us, remembering the words of the Lord: ". . . the Father will give you whatever you ask him in my name" (Jn 15:16). Maybe we wish to pray for our sick niece, or for that problem at work, or maybe for peace in the Middle East.

In the Collect, once we have remembered what it is that we wish to ask God for, the Priest opens his hands in imitation of Jesus' Cross and a venerable sign of prayer called the *orans* position. Then the Priest, acting in the person of Christ, begins to pray the Collect Prayer in the name of the whole People of God and all who are present. Here's the Collect for the night before Christmas:

O God,
who gladden us year by year
as we wait in hope for our redemption,
grant that, just as we joyfully welcome
your Only Begotten son as our Redeemer,
we may also merit to face him confidently
when he comes again as our Judge.
Who lives and reigns with you in the unity of the Holy
     Spirit,
one God, for ever and ever.

If you listen carefully, you will hear how the Collect Prayer consists of three parts. The opening lines praise God, the middle lines ask him for something, and the concluding doxology sums up the prayer by praising the Blessed Trinity.

Finally, the people make the prayer their own by answering "Amen."

Understanding Amen

Each time the Priest prays in the name of the gathered assembly, they respond "Amen." Indeed, Amen is probably the most commonly used word in the prayers of Christianity, Judaism, and Islam. There's an old story of how one day two Christians passed each other on the road, neither of whom knew a word of the other's language. Each recognized that the other was reading the Bible in their own language. So one smiled broadly, proclaiming "Alleluia!" To which the other Christian answered "Amen!"[11]

The word Amen, then, is a wonderful bridge between people separated by religions and even languages, but what does it mean?

Derived from Hebrew, Amen literally means "so be it," but the significance of our Amen is even more than that. Our Amen is the Amen of the Prophet Isaiah, who named God as the "God of the Amen" (65:16), the faithful God, just as in the Book of Revelation, Jesus is given the name "Amen, the faithful one" (cf. 3:14). It is the Amen that accepts God's will, as when the Prophet Jeremiah wrote "Amen! May the LORD do so" (28:6). It is the Amen that desires only that God's will be done.

Finally Amen expresses a desire that all may be fulfilled as God desires it. Like the Blessed Virgin's acceptance of God's will for her, or the martyrs' Amen as they gave their lives to God. May the voices of all who celebrate the Holy Mass, in the words of Saint Ambrose, resound like heavenly thunder to the glory of God![12]

PRAYER[13]

I draw near, loving Lord Jesus Christ,
to the table of your most delightful banquet
in fear and trembling,
a sinner, presuming not upon my own merits,
but trusting rather in your goodness and mercy.

. . . Hail, O Saving Victim,
offered for me and for the whole human race
on the wood of the Cross.
Hail, O noble and precious Blood,
flowing from the wounds
of Jesus Christ, my crucified Lord,
and washing away the sins of all the world.

. . . And grant that this sacred foretaste
of your Body and Blood
which I, though unworthy, intend to receive,
may be the remission of my sins,
the perfect cleansing of my faults,
the banishment of shameful thoughts,
and the rebirth of right sentiments;
and may it encourage
a wholesome and effective performance
of deeds pleasing to you,
and be a most firm defense of body and soul
against the snares of my enemies. Amen.

FOR DISCUSSION

1. How does Mass begin?

2. Discuss the greeting of the people and the altar. How do these differ and how are they the same?

3. How do the Acts of Penitence center on the mercy of Christ? Why not just pray for the forgiveness of our sins?

4. Discuss the origins and current use of the Kyrie.

5. In the Collect, why do we pause after the Priest says "Let us pray"?

6. The "Amen" is the most popular response of the people during Mass. What does it mean and why is it used so often?

Chapter 4

Understanding the Liturgy of the Word

SACRED Scripture is of the greatest importance in the celebration of the liturgy. For it is from it that lessons are read and explained in the homily, and psalms are sung. It is from the Scriptures that the prayers, collects and hymns draw their inspiration and their force, and that actions and signs derive their meaning. (SC 24)

Saint Jerome (340-420), the first person to translate the Bible into the language of the people (it was Latin back then!) used to say, "Not to know the scriptures is not to know Christ."[1]

Hearing the scriptures proclaimed, then, is hearing Christ. They impart without change, the Council Fathers told us, "the Word of God himself and cause the voice of the Holy Spirit to be heard in the words of the apostles and prophets. . . . In the Sacred Books the Father who is in heaven lovingly comes to meet his children and speaks with them."[2]

Our reading, proclaiming, and hearing the Word of God, then, is an intimate encounter between God and his people: it is the Father, speaking his Eternal Word, made flesh in our time, reaching down from heaven into our earthly existence and speaking with us, teaching us the mysteries of life.

While God is present and acting in his word proclaimed, this does not mean that every person who goes
to Mass will be fully converted at each hearing. Yet the
power of the Word is nothing less than the power of
Christ:

> In the celebration of the liturgy the word of God
> is not voiced in only one way nor does it always stir
> the hearts of the hearers with the same efficacy.
> Always, however, Christ is present in his word; as
> he carries out the mystery of salvation, he sancti-
> fies humanity and offers the Father perfect wor-
> ship.[3]

Understanding God's Word

Under the inspiration of the Holy Spirit, the Church
has been given the power to interpret the word of God.
Still, there are many ways to understand the meaning of
the scriptures for our day and age and for us. To truly
understand the scriptures we must join biblical scholars
in studying the meaning of words and concepts in their
original context. This scientific study of the biblical texts
is invaluable for their interpretation and translation into
vernacular languages.

Yet there is an even deeper meaning behind the scrip-
tural texts described in the introduction to the Lectionary
for Mass:

> When in celebrating the Liturgy the Church
> proclaims both the Old and New Testament, it is
> proclaiming one and the same mystery of Christ.

The New Testament lies hidden in the Old; the Old Testament comes fully to light in the New. Christ himself is the center and fullness of the whole of Scripture, just as he is of all liturgical celebration. Thus the Scriptures are the living waters from which all who seek life and salvation must drink.[4]

The eyes of faith, or, as Gregory the Great used to call it, the *oculus amoris,* let us see as one who has witnessed the Resurrection of Jesus, with eyes which recognize that in the light of the paschal mystery all creation has been changed. Such a vision sees the ultimate truth of the Gospel of Christ as hidden within the stories and the histories, the narratives and canticles of the Old Testament.[5]

What Happens in the Liturgy of the Word

We come to Mass to be fed, first from the table of God's word, and then from the table of sacrifice from which we will receive the Body and Blood of Christ. The first part of the Liturgy of the Word is made up of readings from Sacred Scripture, interspersed with chants. This is followed by the Homily, the Creed, and the Universal Prayer (Prayer of the Faithful).

Do you recall the story of the time Jesus read the scriptures in the synagogue in Capernaum? We are told that he walked up the step to the ambo, opened the scrolls and began to read to them from the Prophets about the coming Messiah. "Today," he announced at the conclusion of the reading, "this scripture is fulfilled in your hearing" (Lk 4:21).

At Mass, the lector or Deacon also walks up the step to the ambo, opens the Lectionary, and begins to read the scriptures to us. When they conclude the readings, they announce that what we have heard is God speaking to us!

The ambo is a slightly raised platform on which a lectern, or reading desk, is placed so that all can hear the lector, Deacon, and Priest proclaim the word of God. Only the word of God and certain prayers may be prayed from the ambo.[6]

The First and Second Readings

A lector proclaims the First Reading from scripture, usually taken from the Old Testament.[7] In response to this word we sing a Responsorial Psalm. Then comes the Gospel with its proper acclamation. All these readings are about the same person: Jesus Christ. The Old Testament readings, all written before his birth, foreshadow his coming and are fully understood only in the light of his Gospel. The readings from the epistles and the Acts of the Apostles were written after his crucifixion. They continue the teaching of his apostles in those first years after he died and rose to save us.

The Word of the Lord!

After each of these readings, the lector announces proudly, "The word of the Lord!" and we respond, "Thanks be to God!" At the end of the Gospel, the Deacon proclaims, "The Gospel of the Lord!" and we respond, "Praise to you, Lord Jesus Christ!"

All of these acclamations are unambiguous and in the present tense. The Lord is present and active and speaking to us in his word proclaimed! Christ is standing in our midst, and we can hear him as clearly as the disciples did when he walked the roads of Jerusalem with them.

For what we have heard is nothing less than God speaking to us. It is the lector's voice, but God's own word: Christ present in his own word, who proclaims the Gospel.[8] "Christ does not speak in the past, but in the present, even as he is present in the liturgical action."[9]

Yet, we seem too often to forget this great good news. Too often, the Liturgy of the Word becomes repetitive or perfunctory, even for the lectors who are proclaiming the scriptures! Imagine if Christ were to appear at the local stadium in your town. How the crowds would rush to hear him! Yet he is truly present and he can be truly heard speaking a word for this people in this time and place at every celebration of the Mass.

Perhaps this is because we think of listening as passive and benign. But there is nothing benign about God revealing to us the meaning of life. And there is nothing passive in hearing the message of the one who made us, died and rose for us, and speaks to us still through his word proclaimed. Such listening, as Pope John Paul II once taught us, is really profoundly active. Yet, regrettably it may be true that "in a culture which neither favors nor fosters meditative quiet, the art of interior listening is learned only with difficulty."[10]

The Responsorial Psalm

A response to the readings in the form of a sung Psalm was not uncommon in the synagogues of Jesus' day. Today's Responsorial Psalm is a descendant of this practice. In the earliest days, this Psalm was often sung from the first step *(gradus)* of the ambo, rather than from the reading table at the top of the elevated platform. Thus did its name come to be known simply as *the Gradual.*

The Gospel

Finally, we come to the high point of the Liturgy of the Word: the Gospel. While the Church holds all the scriptures in the highest esteem, the Gospels have always held a preeminent place in the Liturgy as containing the very words of Christ.[11] This is why the Gospel is always accompanied by special marks of honor. The Deacon alone, or in his absence, the Priest, may proclaim the Gospel. Oftentimes the reading of the Gospel is preceded by a procession with the *Book of the Gospels,* accompanied by candles and incense, and there are a special introductory dialogue and rituals accompanying its proclamation.

The Book of the Gospels

Venerated above all the books used in the Liturgy, the *Book of the Gospels* is, along with the altar, a primary sign of the presence of Christ in the liturgical assembly. This is why we kiss the altar and the *Book of the Gospels,* and why the *Book of the Gospels* is carried in procession from altar to ambo, as a sign of Christ coming into our midst. The *Book of the Gospels* also plays a special role in the rites for the ordination of a Bishop and Deacons and is enthroned at synods and councils of the Church as a sign that Christ is presiding over these holy assemblies.

Traditionally, the *Book of the Gospels* is among the most richly ornamented of all the sacred objects used in the Liturgy. Often it will carry an image of the Risen Christ in glory or of the Evangelists in silver or ivory.

The Gospel Procession and Acclamation

The proclamation of the Gospel begins with a procession that marks the coming of Christ. After he has received the Priest's blessing, the Deacon brings the *Book of the Gospels* to the ambo. In this procession we see Christ entering into our midst, not unlike the children who lined his way with palm branches when he gloriously entered Jerusalem before his saving Passion and Death. This procession is accompanied by our most joyous chant, the *Alleluia*, that has been sung since Christ first rose from the tomb. Ministers with incense and candles also accompany the procession.

As the procession moves from altar to ambo, the Alleluia chant is sung.[12] The Alleluia (meaning Praise YHWH or Praise the Lord!) dates from the time of the first Temple in Jerusalem. Several of the Temple Psalms employ an Alleluia at the beginning and the end, probably as a common response for those in procession to the Temple mount. The only time the word is used in the New Testament, however, is in some manuscript traditions of the hymn of the victorious saints enjoying the beatific vision in the Kingdom of Heaven (Rev 19:1-7). This passage still serves as a hymn at Evening Prayer on Sunday evenings:

Salvation, glory, and power to our God: Alleluia;
his judgments are honest and true: Alleluia.

Sing praise to our God, all you his servants:
    Alleluia;
all who worship him reverently great and small:
    Alleluia.

The Lord our all powerful God is King: Alleluia;
let us rejoice, sing praise, and give him glory:
    Alleluia.

The wedding feast of the Lamb has begun:
    Alleluia;
and his bride is prepared to welcome him:
    Alleluia.

This repeated singing of the Alleluia to verses from
the canticle is not only similar to the use of the Alleluia
processions to the Temple but practically identical to the
chant which accompanies the procession of the *Book of
the Gospels.*

The *Book of the Gospels* represents Christ. Indeed,
just as we kiss the altar, because it is a primary sign of the
presence of Christ, so do we kiss the Gospel Book for the
same reason.

Just as the Alleluias were sung in the procession to
God's Temple in former times, and just as we will sing the
same Alleluia when Christ the Lamb takes his throne in
heaven, so we sing Alleluias to welcome the King of
Glory as he comes to speak to us in the words of his Holy
Gospel.

Proclamation of the Gospel

When the Deacon reaches the ambo, he greets the people with the same greeting used by the Priest: *The Lord be with you.* The people respond, and, while he makes the Sign of the Cross on the Gospel, he proclaims: *A reading from the holy Gospel According to (Evangelist).* As all respond, *Glory to you, O Lord!,* all make the Sign of the Cross on their forehead, their lips, and their heart in a silent prayer "that the Word might enlighten their minds, cleanse their hearts, and open their lips, to proclaim the praise of the Lord."[13] If incense is used, the Deacon then incenses the *Book of the Gospels.*

The Homily

In the Homily or sermon, the Priest (sometimes the Deacon gives the homily) gives nourishment to our lives by explaining some aspect of the readings we have heard, the particular mystery we are celebrating, or one of the parts of the Mass.

> My mother went to church twice a day; she went in the morning and the evening without ever allowing anything to keep her away, and she went not to hear idle tales and the gossip of old women, but that she might hear you, O Lord, in your homilies, and that you might hear her in her prayers.[14]

Thus Saint Augustine describes his mother's twice a day visit to church. For two tasks did Monica make her morning and evening pilgrimage. Not "to hear idle tales and the gossip of old women" but to pray and to be nourished by the word of God. And curiously enough, that nourishment was received through the Homily.

Not unlike the respondents to contemporary studies of parish life, Monica sought her essential nourishment in that place where, as the new *Lectionary for Mass* describes it, "the spoken word of God and the liturgy of the Eucharist [are brought] together [to] become 'a proclamation of God's wonderful works in the history of salvation, the mystery of Christ.' "[15]

And whose proclamation are these homilies? They are described as "your homilies, O Lord" in which Monica hears "you, O Lord." Not Ambrose's homilies! Not the Church's homilies! But the homilies of the Lord, not unlike the proclamation we so often utter and so seldom believe: "This is the Word of the Lord!"

For Augustine then, and for his pious mother, the homily was Christ speaking, Christ present and active in his Church—Christ feeding his people with his word. May it be the same for us today!

Creed

Then follows the Profession of Faith, or Creed. On Sundays and major feasts, we respond to God's word by professing our belief in the great mysteries of our faith . . . reciting together "the rule of faith."[16]

Either of two creeds may be professed at Mass. The older of them, the Apostles' Creed, was once attributed to the Apostles themselves and has its origins in the professions of the Rite of Baptism. It is particularly appropriate during the Easter season, when we recall our Baptism.

The Apostles' Creed also forms the outline for the summary of the Church's belief in the *Catechism of the Catholic Church*.

The Nicene Creed has its origins with the Council of Nicaea in the fourth century, but did not take its final form for more than a century. It contains the most succinct summary of what we believe as Catholics. While many of its teachings are hard, at first, to understand, Catholics should strive throughout their lives to open their hearts and their minds to the revealed truth it contains.

When the Nicene Creed is proclaimed, all bow from the waist at the words *and by the Holy Spirit . . . became man*; but on the solemnities of the Annunciation and of the Nativity of the Lord, all genuflect. An ancient tradition also suggests that all bow at mention of the incarnation of Jesus Christ as man.

NICENE CREED:

I believe in one God, the Father Almighty,
maker of heaven and earth,
of all things visible and invisible.
I believe in one Lord Jesus Christ,
the Only Begotten Son of God,
born of the Father before all ages.
God from God, Light from Light,
true God from true God,
begotten, not made, consubstantial with the Father;
through him all things were made.
For us men and for our salvation he came down from
     heaven,

at the words that follow, up to and including **and became man**, *all bow.*

and by the Holy Spirit was incarnate of the Virgin Mary,

and became man.

For our sake he was crucified under Pontius Pilate,

he suffered death and was buried,

and rose again on the third day in accordance with the scriptures.

He ascended into heaven

and is seated at the right hand of the Father.

He will come again in glory to judge the living and the dead

and his kingdom will have no end.

I believe in the Holy Spirit, the Lord, the giver of life,

who proceeds from the Father and the Son,

who with the Father and the Son is adored and glorified,

who has spoken through the prophets.

I believe in one, holy, catholic and apostolic church.

I confess one Baptism for the forgiveness of sins

and I look forward to the resurrection of the dead

and the life of the world to come. Amen.

APOSTLES' CREED:

I believe in God,

the Father almighty,

creator of heaven and earth,

and in Jesus Christ, his only Son, our Lord,

at the words that follow, up to and including **the Virgin Mary,** *all bow.*

who was conceived by the Holy Spirit,
born of the Virgin Mary,
suffered under Pontius Pilate,
was crucified, died and was buried;
he descended into hell;
on the third day he rose again from the dead;
he ascended into heaven,
and is seated at the right hand of God the Father Almighty;
from there he will come to judge the living and the dead.

I believe in the Holy Spirit,
the holy catholic church,
the communion of saints, the forgiveness of sins,
the resurrection of the body, and life everlasting. Amen.

Universal Prayer or Prayer of the Faithful

Because "the joy and hope, the struggle and anguish of the people of this age and especially of the poor and those suffering in any way are the joy and hope, the struggle and anguish of Christ's disciples,[17] the Church prays not just for its own needs but for the salvation of the world, for civil authorities, for those oppressed by any burden, and for the local community, particularly those who are sick or who have died."[18]

The Prayer of the Faithful has been a part of our Liturgy for a very long time. In fact, Saint Augustine would frequently end his homilies in the fourth century by saying: "Turning to the Lord, let us pray to him for ourselves and all of his people who are here with us in this house, that he may deign to guard and protect them."

So do we respond to God's word by making our needs known to him. In the Universal Prayer (Prayer of the Faithful), those gathered offer prayers for the salvation of all by virtue of their baptismal priesthood.

After the Priest has called everyone to prayer, intentions are announced and responded to for the Church, civil authorities, those in need, and for the salvation of the whole world. The prayers are concluded with a prayer by the Priest, asking God to look on the needs that have been proclaimed.

From Word to Eucharist

Having listened to God's word and received the gift of a deeper and stronger faith (cf. Rom 10:17), we now prepare to receive the word made flesh as spiritual food.

PRAYER[19]

Soul of Christ, sanctify me.
Body of Christ, save me.
Blood of Christ, embolden me.
Water from the side of Christ, wash me.
Passion of Christ, strengthen me.
O good Jesus, hear me.
Within your wounds hide me.
Never permit me to be parted from you.
From the evil Enemy defend me.

At the hour of my death call me
and bid me come to you,
that with your Saints I may praise you
for age upon age.
Amen.

FOR DISCUSSION

1. Discuss the acclamation at the end of the readings: "The word of the Lord."

2. What does it mean that the New Testament can help us to understand the Old Testament?

3. How is the ministry of the lector today similar to what Jesus did when he read from the scrolls in the synagogue in Capernaum?

4. What does it mean that the altar and the ambo are two tables?

5. How is the proclamation of the Gospel different from the proclamation of the other biblical readings?

6. When is it usually more appropriate to use the Apostles' Creed rather than the Nicene Creed?

7. How is the Prayer of the Faithful a "universal prayer"?

Chapter 5

Understanding the Liturgy of the Eucharist

At the Last Supper, on the night when He was betrayed, our Savior instituted the Eucharistic sacrifice of His Body and Blood. He did this in order to perpetuate the sacrifice of the Cross throughout the centuries until He should come again, and so to entrust to His beloved spouse, the Church, a memorial of His death and resurrection: a sacrament of love, a sign of unity, a bond of charity, *a paschal banquet in which Christ is eaten, the mind is filled with grace, and a pledge of future glory is given to us.*[1]

These are the same words used by the Church today to describe what happens in the second half of the Mass:[2] "a Paschal Sacrifice and banquet, by which the Sacrifice of the Cross is continuously made present in the Church whenever the Priest, representing Christ the Lord, carries out what the Lord himself did and handed over to his disciples to be done in his memory."[3]

Do you remember the words that Jesus spoke at the Last Supper? At the end of the meal he took bread, blessed it, broke it, and said, "Take this all of you and eat it, for this is my body which will be given up for you." At the end of the meal he took the cup filled with wine, and said, "Take this, all of you, and drink from it. For this is the cup of my blood, the blood of the new and everlasting covenant which will be given up for you. Do this in memory of me."

From the first Masses of the Apostles in the Upper Room of Jerusalem, this is the way the Eucharist has been celebrated. Jesus said, "take this . . . ," and so we take bread and wine and place them on the altar. Jesus blessed the bread, and so the Priest gives thanks for the gift of salvation in the great Eucharistic Prayer, and the gifts of bread and wine become the Body and Blood of Christ. Jesus broke the bread and gave it to his disciples. So the Priest breaks the bread which has become Christ's Body, so that we, though many, may "receive from the one bread the Lord's Body and from the one chalice the Lord's Blood in the same way the Apostles received them from Christ's own hands."[4]

The Liturgy of the Eucharist, then, has three main parts: the Preparation of the Gifts, the Eucharistic Prayer, and the Communion Rite.

The Preparation of the Gifts

AFTER the Liturgy of the Word has concluded with the Universal Prayer, all are seated for the Preparation of the Gifts.

Presentation of the Gifts

Once the altar has been prepared with the corporal, purificator, Missal, and chalice, a few of the faithful bring forward offerings of bread and wine and present them to the Priest. This Procession with the Gifts is accompanied by the Offertory chant or song.

Once these gifts of bread and wine came from the kitchens of those who brought them to Mass. Sometimes, each one present brought forth bread and wine, with the surplus going to the poor. Today, the bread and wine are usually purchased by the parish, and instead we bring forth gifts of money in support of the needs of the Church and the poor.

But the Procession with the Gifts still has a profound meaning. For the gathered faithful are not silent spectators at what the Priest does on their behalf. Those gathered here by Christ form a chosen race, a royal priesthood, a holy nation, God's own people,[5] joining the sacrifices of their lives with the one and perfect sacrifice of Christ upon the Cross.

When gifts of bread and wine are placed into the hands of the Priest, it is not just bread that is offered, but with those pieces of bread are mixed all the sacrifices of our lives. And with the wine in that cruet are mixed the joys and sorrows, the longings and holy desires of each member of the gathered assembly. At this presentation the faithful are like the Magi bringing gifts to the Christ child. But these gifts are of an even greater value than gold, frankincense, and myrrh, for these are the gifts of our lives.

The French poet Paul Claudel[6] once wrote of this moment:

> Your prayers, and your faith, and your blood, with His in the chalice.
> These, like the water and wine, form the matter of his sacrifice.

Or, as Cardinal Suhard wrote over a hundred years ago:

> When you approach the altar, never come alone. Together with yourselves, you have the power and the mission to save your home, your street, your city, and the whole of civilization. . . . The worker will offer up the monotony of assembly-line work or the joy of skilled craftsmanship. The mother of a family will offer up her household cares, her fears for a sick child. The man of science will offer up the world of ideas, the universe whose depth and breadth have been tapped. It is the task of the scholar, the philosopher, the sociologist, the artist, at this turning point in the world's history, to gather the world together in order to raise it up to the Father.[7]

We place those gifts into the hands of the Priest, offering them to Christ. Then the Priest, acting in the person of Christ, places those gifts upon the altar in the same way that Christ placed his body upon the altar of the Cross in a perfect sacrifice of praise. These are the gifts that will be transformed by the great Eucharistic Prayer into the very Body and Blood of Christ, and then returned to us as our nourishment that we might have the strength to continue to join ourselves with Christ's sacrifice every day of our lives.

Not only gifts of bread and wine, of course, but monetary donations to support the work of the Church and to assist those who are poor are likewise collected inspired by Christ "who became poor to make us rich."[8]

Those who are well off, and who are also willing, give as each chooses. What is gathered is given to him who presides to assist orphans and widows, those whom illness or any other cause has deprived of resources, prisoners, immigrants and, in a word, all who are in need.[9]

Prayer over the Gifts

The Priest places these gifts upon the altar, while praying certain prayers. On more solemn occasions, the gifts, the altar and the cross are incensed in order to signify that the Church's offerings and prayers rise up like incense in the sight of God.[10] The Priest and the people may also be incensed. This is because the Priest offers the Sacrifice of the altar, even as the gathered faithful have offered the sacrifices of their lives.

As the Priest places the gifts upon the altar he holds them in his hands, just a little above the mensa (altar table). He does not raise the gifts in offering, as at the doxology of the Eucharistic Prayer. Nor does he raise them up for everyone to see as at the Consecration or the *Ecce Agne Dei*. Here he simply takes them into his hands in the same manner that the Lord would have done each time he took bread at the beginning of a meal with his disciples to bless God and the food they were about to eat.

> **Blessed are you, Lord God of all creation,**
> **for through your goodness we have received the bread we offer you:**
> **fruit of the earth and work of human hands,**
> **it will become for us the bread of life.**

Then the Priest places the paten with the bread on the corporal.

The people acclaim:

Blessed be God for ever.

Then the Deacon, or the Priest, pours wine and a little water into the chalice, saying quietly:

> **By the mystery of this water and wine may we come to share in the divinity of Christ who humbled himself to share in our humanity.**

The Priest then takes the chalice and holds it slightly raised above the altar with both hands, saying in a low voice:

Blessed are you, Lord God of all creation,
for through your goodness we have received the wine
**   we offer you:**
fruit of the vine and work of human hands,
it will become our spiritual drink.

Then he places the chalice on the corporal.

Then the Priest washes his hands at the side of the altar, while praying a verse from Psalm 51:2, asking that God might cleanse him from all his sins in order that he might be worthy to offer this great sacrifice.[11]

The Suscipiat and the Prayer over the Offerings

The Preparation of the Gifts is concluded by two prayers. First, the Priest asks the faithful to pray for him "that my sacrifice and yours may be acceptable to God the Almighty Father."

What does the Priest mean when he asks us to pray that his sacrifice and ours might be acceptable to God? His sacrifice is the one that only a Priest can offer. Our sacrifices are the ones that we have presented with the gifts of bread and wine, and that are now joined to the perfect sacrifice of Calvary. So the people respond by standing and praying for the Priest:

All: **May the Lord accept the sacrifice at your hands,**
for the praise and glory of his name,
for our good and the good of all his holy Church.

This is the one instance during the Mass when the Priest stands silent as the people respond as a Royal Priesthood, praying that God accept the sacrifice at the hands of the Priest "for our good, and the good of all his Church."

Then the Priest prays one final Prayer over the Offerings by which he asks God to receive our gifts and give to us the Body and Blood of his Son. Many of these prayers recall the irony first indicated by Saint Augustine: that the gifts we give to God were first received from him, and that by now receiving our gifts, he will give to us his very self.

Prayer over the Offerings (December 29)

Receive our oblation, O Lord,
by which is brought about a glorious exchange,
that by offering what you have given
we may merit to receive your very self.

As in the Collect Prayer, the people signify their agreement by answering "Amen."

The Eucharistic Prayer

The "center and summit" of the entire Mass now takes place. The Priest prays for and with the People of God and all present.

While there are four Eucharistic Prayers used at most Masses, and six more that may be used on special occasions, they all follow the same structure, which reveals an "inexhaustible theological and spiritual richness."[12]

The Introductory Dialogue

The Eucharistic Prayer begins with a dialogue between Priest and people by which all prepare themselves for this great prayer. It dates from the time of the Apostolic Tradition (215 A.D.) and has remained unchanged throughout the centuries. First, the Priest greets the people with the same greeting he used to greet us at the beginning of Mass and to call us to prayer for the Collect:

Priest: **The Lord be with you.**

People: **And with your spirit.**

Next the Priest speaks to the people in words and gestures at the same time. He urges them to lift up their hearts and to join them with Christ and with him to prepare to offer a sacrifice of thanksgiving and praise to God the Father. The dialogue, one of the oldest recorded exchanges at Mass, invites us to enter into the most sacred action of the Liturgy by making the journey with Christ from this world to the Father (cf. Jn 13), who reigns on high and is the object of our prayer. Simultaneously, the Priest raises his arms, as if to physically urge the hearts of the people to be lifted up to God:

Priest: **Lift up your hearts!**

People: **We lift them up to the Lord!**

The Fathers of the Church, from Cyprian to Augustine, frequently commented on this dialogue. It is something like a call to all creation: to every creature who has grown weary or whose heart has grown heavy with the care of the world to reach deep within their innermost selves and lift their hearts up to the Lord, joining them to the perfect sacrifice of praise of Christ upon the altar of the Cross!

This introductory dialogue concludes with an invitation and response that would have been known as a part of the Jewish Liturgy in the time of Jesus. Yet no one can doubt that the call to offer thanks takes on special significance in this, the highpoint of all prayers of thanksgiving, the Eucharistic Prayer.

Finally, he invites all present to join him in offering the Eucharistic Prayer, to which the people respond with an ancient Roman juridical formula, sealing and approving of his intent:

Priest: **Let us give thanks to the Lord our God.**

People: **It is right and just.**

The Preface

The Introductory Dialogue leads into the Preface, for which all remain standing. Here, in the name of the entire

People of God, the Priest gives thanks for all that God has done for us. The text of the Preface frequently changes throughout the liturgical year in reflecting on the particular dimensions of the mystery of Christ and the saints whom we happen to be celebrating. The texts we will use for this study are taken from the Second Eucharistic Prayer:

> **It is truly right and just, our duty and our salvation,**
> **always and everywhere to give you thanks,**
> **Father most holy, through your beloved Son, Jesus**
> **   Christ,**
> **your Word through whom you made all things,**
> **whom you sent as our Savior and Redeemer,**
> **incarnate by the Holy Spirit and born of the Virgin.**
>
> **Fulfilling your will and gaining for you a holy people,**
> **he stretched out his hands as he endured his Passion,**
> **so as to break the bonds of death and manifest the**
> **   resurrection.**
> **and so, with the Angels and all the Saints**
> **we declare your glory, as with one voice we acclaim:**

The Preface concludes with an ancient acclamation, the *Sanctus (Holy, Holy . . .),* in which heaven and earth join their voices in praise of God's glory:

> **Holy, Holy, Holy Lord, God of hosts,**
> **Heaven and earth are full of your glory.**
> **Hosanna in the highest.**
> **Blessed is he who comes in the name of the Lord.**
> **Hosanna in the highest.**

The *Sanctus* acclamation, which is sung at the end of the Preface, begins with a text from the first four verses of chapter six of the Book of the Prophet Isaiah, told in the Prophet's own voice:

> In the year that King Uzziah died, I saw the Lord sitting on a throne, high and lofty; and the hem of his robe filled the temple. Seraphs were in attendance above him; each had six wings: with two they covered their faces, and with two they covered their feet, and with two they flew. And one called to another and said:
>
> **"Holy, holy, holy is the LORD of hosts;**
> **the whole earth is full of his glory."**
>
> The pivots on the thresholds shook at the voices of those who called, and the house was filled with smoke.

With the singing of the *Sanctus* we realize that the Eucharistic Prayer is about to be an extraordinary event. It is a prayer that transcends the boundaries of time and space. The moment of Christ's Death on a hill outside Jerusalem is about to become a moment in this day's Mass in our parish church. The voices of the choir and the old couple behind me are about to be blended with the choirs of angels and the saints. In the Eucharistic Prayer, then, the Kingdom of Heaven is already, but not yet, and the Lord Jesus returns to us in his Body and Blood—just as he will at the end of time.

After several centuries of use in Palestinian synagogue worship, the *Sanctus* received its present form

with the addition of the words of the crowds as Jesus
entered the city of Jerusalem that heralded his saving
Passion and Death a few days later:

> When they drew near Jerusalem and had
> reached Bethphage on the Mount of Olives, Jesus
> sent off two disciples, saying to them, "Go to the vil-
> lage directly ahead of you, and as soon as you enter
> you will find a tethered donkey and a colt with her.
> Untie them and bring them to me." . . . The disciples
> went off and did as Jesus had instructed them. They
> brought the donkey and the colt, and laid their
> cloaks on their backs, and he sat on them. A very
> large crowd spread their cloaks on the road, while
> others cut branches from the trees and spread them
> on the road. The crowds that preceded him and
> those that followed kept shouting:

> "Hosanna to the Son of David!
> Blessed is he who comes in the name of the Lord!
> Hosanna in the highest!"

> And when he entered Jerusalem, the whole city
> was filled with excitement. "Who is this?" the people
> asked, and the crowds replied, "This is the prophet
> Jesus from Nazareth in Galilee" (Mt 21:1-2, 6-11; cf.
> Ps 117:26).

To the voices of the angels and saints, then, we add the
song of triumphal entry into Jerusalem, a journey that is
also the Christ's entry into his Passion and Death. His
coming to us is always by way of the Cross and the glo-

rious banquet is always celebrated in the light of his Paschal sacrifice. Thus we are able to sing with one and the same voice: "Blessed is he who comes in the name of the Lord! Hosanna in the highest!"

After the *Sanctus* has been sung, the thanksgiving continues, albeit very briefly in the Second Eucharistic Prayer:

You are indeed Holy, O Lord,
the fount of all holiness.

The Epiclesis

Immediately thereafter, the Priest asks the Father to send his Spirit down upon the gifts of bread and wine, joining his hands in a gesture of descent and imposition. He also prays that the gifts of bread and wine be changed into Christ's Body and Blood.[13]

Make holy, therefore, these gifts,
we pray,
by sending down your Spirit upon them
like the dewfall,
so that they may become for us
the Body and Blood of our Lord Jesus Christ

In the homilies that he preached to the newly Baptized in fourth-century Jerusalem, Saint Cyril reflects on the action of the Holy Spirit in the epiclesis, recalling that at Mass we:

. . . call upon God in his mercy to send his Holy Spirit upon the offerings before us, to transform the bread into the body of Christ and the wine into the blood of Christ. Whatever the Holy Spirit touches is sanctified and completely transformed.[14]

And yet not only the gifts of bread and wine are transformed, but we who received Christ's Body and Blood are gathered by the Holy Spirit "into one body" being made a spiritual offering to the Father.[15]

The Consecration

Then the Priest recalls the very words of Jesus at the Last Supper. This moment is often referred to as the consecration, since no less a commentator than Saint Ambrose proclaimed that by these words the bread and wine truly become the Body and Blood of Christ. These words, along with the calling down of the Holy Spirit, are the central actions of the Eucharistic sacrifice.

The Priest begins by recalling:

**At the time he was betrayed
and entered willingly into his Passion,**

A similar reference to the Passion begins the consecration in each of the Eucharistic Prayers. This is because the words and actions of the Lord's Supper draw their power from and lead us to the sacrifice of Calvary. Thus the sacrifice of the altar and the sacrifice of the Cross are one and the same.

Then the Priest takes the host in his hands, and, raising the bread a little above the altar, says:

**he took bread and, giving thanks,
broke it, and gave it to his disciples, saying:**

The Priest then bows slightly and says the same words which Jesus spoke at the Last Supper:

Take this, all of you, and eat of it,
for this is my Body,
which will be given up for you.

He shows the consecrated host to the people, places it back on the paten, and genuflects in adoration.

Our brief reflection on the words of consecration give us the opportunity to recall what they really say. Jesus did not say, "This is a symbol of my body," or "This will remind you of my body." Jesus said, "This is my Body, which will be given up for you." In the Blessed Sacrament, then, Jesus is as truly present as he was when he ate with the disciples after his Resurrection.

This is why, when the Priest shows the consecrated host to the gathered assembly, a bell is sometimes rung, and on occasion, the consecrated host is incensed. Just as at his incarnation, we can almost hear the angels sing: *Venite adoremus!* Come, let us adore him!

Then the Priest does the same for the words that Jesus spoke over the chalice. Taking the chalice filled with wine into his hands, he recalls:

In a similar way, when supper was ended,

The Priest takes the chalice, raises it a bit off the altar, bows slightly, and, just as he did for the bread, recalls the words which Jesus spoke at the Last Supper:

he took the chalice
and, once more giving thanks,

he gave it to his disciples, saying:

Take this all of you, and drink from it:
this is the chalice of my Blood,
the Blood of the new and everlasting covenant.
which will be shed for you and for many
for the forgiveness of sins.

Do this in memory of me.

Just as he did for the consecrated host, the Priest then shows to the people the chalice, now holding Christ's own Precious Blood, sometimes with the accompaniment of bells and incense. Then he returns the chalice to the altar and genuflects in adoration.

The Anamnesis

Immediately after the Consecration, the Priest proclaims "The mystery of faith!" These words, which used to be included in the words of institution, are now used as a proclamation of the saving sacrifice that has just been celebrated in the consecration of the Bread and Wine. The response of the people to this acclamation of the Eucharistic mystery is a proclamation of their incorporation into this great Paschal Mystery. Each of the acclamations are addressed to Christ, now present upon the altar:

We proclaim your death, O Lord,
and profess your Resurrection
until you come again.

or:

When we eat this Bread and drink this Cup,
we proclaim your Death, O Lord,
until you come again.

or:

Save us, Savior of the world,
for by your Cross and Resurrection
you have set us free.

The Offering

The Priest continues with the anamnesis, as "the Church expounds "the Passion, resurrection, and glorious return of Christ Jesus" [16] that we have just proclaimed in the Mystery of Faith. The gathered liturgical assembly "presents to the Father the offering of his Son which reconciles us with him"[17] and reaffirms participation in it along with the whole Church. In this, they offer their lives along with Christ, the spotless Victim, to God the Father.

Therefore, as we celebrate the memorial of his Death
and Resurrection,
we offer you, Lord,
the Bread of life and the Chalice of salvation,
giving thanks that you have held us worthy
to be in your presence and minister to you.

Humbly we pray that,
partaking of the Body and Blood of Christ,
we may be gathered into one by the Holy Spirit.

The Intercessions

Then prayers are offered for the Church in heaven and on earth: for the living and the dead and for all those who are in need. In particular, we pray for the Pope and the Bishop by name. In some of the Eucharistic Prayers the names of others who are in need or the names of the deceased are said aloud by the Priest.

Remember, Lord, your Church, spread throughout the world,
and bring her to the fullness of charity,
together with *N*. our Pope and *N*. our Bishop and all the clergy.

Prayers for those who have died at this moment in the Liturgy are of particular importance. As Catholics, we believe that the Mass can bring spiritual benefit to those who have died. Saint Augustine reminds us of the tradition "handed down from the Fathers, that prayers should be offered for those who have died in the communion of the Body and Blood of Christ, when they are commemorated in their proper place at the Sacrifice."[18]

Remember also our brothers and sisters
who have fallen asleep in the hope of the resurrection,
and all who have died in your mercy:
welcome them into the light of your face.

The *Catechism of the Catholic* Church speaks explicitly of the need to pray for the dead whose souls await the beatific vision in Purgatory:

> From the beginning the Church has honored the memory of the dead and offered prayers in suffrage for them, above all the Eucharistic sacrifice, so that, thus purified, they may attain the beatific vision of God. The Church also commends almsgiv-

ing, indulgences, and works of penance undertaken on behalf of the dead: Let us help and commemorate them. . . .[19]

These prayers of intercession are always made in communion with the Saints, and especially Mary, the Mother of God and the Apostles. In the oldest and first of the Eucharistic Prayers, a long list of thirty-nine Saints whose intercession we rely on is recited. The list includes the Apostles, the earliest Popes (all of whom were martyrs) and Saints who have been prayed to frequently since the earliest days of the Church.

Have mercy on us all, we pray,
that with the Blessed Virgin Mary, Mother of God,
with the blessed Apostles,
and all the Saints who have pleased you throughout
the ages,
we may merit to be coheirs to eternal life,
and may praise and glorify you
through your Son, Jesus Christ.

Final Doxology

The Eucharistic Prayer concludes with a Trinitarian praise of the Glory of God, sealed with the acclamation of the faithful.

Through him, and with him, and in him,
O God, almighty Father,
in the unity of the Holy Spirit,
all glory and honor is yours,
for ever and ever. Amen.

The doxology asks that through, with, and in Christ, all glory and honor might be given to God in the Holy Spirit. Acting as a seal and affirmation of the whole Eucharistic Prayer by the gathered faithful, the "Great Amen" which concludes the doxology has always been seen as among the most solemn acclamations of the people at Mass. Indeed, when in the third century there arose a dispute concerning the need to rebaptize those who had been initiated into heretical sects, at least one commentator suggested that they should be considered fully Catholic because they "had listened to the Eucharistic Prayer and joined in the Amen."[20]

The Communion Rite

The Lord's Prayer

The Communion Rite begins with an invitation from the Priest to pray the most familiar of all the prayers, the one that the Lord Jesus himself taught us:

**At the Savior's command
and formed by divine teaching,
we dare to say:**

**Our Father, who art in heaven,
hallowed be thy name;
thy kingdom come,
thy will be done on earth as it is in heaven.
Give us this day our daily bread,
and forgive us our trespasses,
as we forgive those who trespass against us;**

**and lead us not into temptation,
but deliver us from evil.**

As we pray the "Our Father" our request for "daily bread" takes on new meaning in the light of the Bread of Life which we are about to receive. "The Eucharist is our daily bread. Its effect is that we may become what we receive. Our daily bread is also the reading you hear and the hymns you sing in church. All are necessities for our pilgrimage."[21]

Likewise, our prayer to be delivered from evil and saved from temptation helps us as we prepare ourselves for the reception of Holy Communion. In a fourth-century sermon, Saint Augustine stresses how these intercessions allow us to "approach the altar with clean faces; with clean faces we share in the body and blood of Christ."[22]

After the faithful have recited the Lord's Prayer, the Priest expands upon its last four words: "deliver us from evil."

**Deliver us, Lord, we pray, from every evil,
graciously grant peace in our days,
that, by the help of your mercy,
we may be always free from sin
and safe from all distress,
as we await the blessed hope
and the coming of our Savior, Jesus Christ.**

The prayer suggests that should we be delivered from evil and consequently kept free from sin, we will know peace in our day and peace in our hearts. Such a peace is not an end in itself, however, but is part of the quickening expectation of the coming of the Lord Jesus at the end of time, which we await, in the words of Saint Paul's Letter to Titus, "with joyful hope."

The prayer concludes with an ancient doxology associated with the Lord's Prayer since the time of the *Didache*. Indeed, the acclamation is associated with some biblical manuscripts and was, therefore, adopted by the Protestant reformers in all forms of recitation of the Lord's Prayer. In the Mass, it is prayed at this point by the entire gathered assembly:

For the kingdom,
the power and the glory are yours
now and for ever.

The Rite of Peace

The Lord's Prayer is followed by the Rite of Peace, at the heart of which is a prayer to the Lord Jesus, recalling how when he appeared to his disciples in the Upper Room after the Resurrection his first words to them were "Peace be with you."

Lord Jesus Christ, who said to your Apostles:
Peace I leave you, my peace I give you,
look not on our sins, but on the faith of your Church,
and graciously grant her peace and unity
in accordance with your will.
Who live and reign for ever and ever.
The people respond: **Amen.**

So we ask the Lord Jesus to deliver us from all anxiety and to grant us that peace which the world cannot give. After the Priest concludes the prayer, he wishes all present the peace of Christ, and then all offer it to those who are standing around them.

The Fraction

Having prepared the gifts and prayed the great Eucharistic Prayer, we now come to one of the most ancient rites of the Mass: the Breaking of the Bread. Such importance had been given to this action by the Lord at the Last Supper that one of the most popular names for the Mass in the New Testament is "the Breaking of the Bread."

Saint Paul, in writing to the Church at Corinth, reflects on the meaning of the fraction:

> The bread that we break, is it not a sharing in the Body of Christ? Because there is one bread, we who are many are one body, for we all partake of the one bread (1 Cor 10:16b-17).

The *Didache*, a first-century compilation of Church traditions, picks up on the same theme in a verse which has become a popular contemporary Catholic hymn:

> As grain once scattered on the hillsides,
> was in this broken bread made one,
> So from all lands thy Church be gathered
> into thy kingdom by thy Son.

Similarly, Saint Peter reminds us that by the brokenness of the one who bore our sins upon the Cross, we have been healed (1 Pt 2:24).

The Priest breaks the bread into pieces so that all might receive from the one loaf, "the many made one body in Christ."[23]

While the Breaking of the Bread is taking place, the Agnus Dei is sung, asking the Lamb who takes away the sins of the world (remember when we sang this in the Gloria?) to have mercy on us, and finally, to grant us his peace.

Lamb of God, you take away the sins of the world, have mercy on us.

Lamb of God, you take away the sins of the world, have mercy on us.

Lamb of God, you take away the sins of the world, grant us peace.

Since the end of the seventh century, the Agnus Dei has been sung during the Breaking of the Bread at Mass. Jesus is the Lamb of God, the name first given him by Saint John the Baptist on the day of his Baptism in the Jordan River. He is the Paschal Lamb, sacrificed for our sins. His flesh is the food which gives us the strength for our exodus from slavery and our journey to the promised land, while his blood delivers us from death. He is the Victorious Lamb, of whom the Book of Revelation speaks, who from his throne in the heavenly Jerusalem is the hope of the Saints, now freed from sin, for they have washed their robes in his Blood and have become whiter than snow (cf. Rev 22:14).

After he breaks the bread, the Priest breaks a small piece of the host and drops it into the Precious Blood while praying quietly:

May this mingling of the Body and Blood
of our Lord Jesus Christ
bring eternal life to us who receive it.

This ancient rite has come to signify the unity of the Body and Blood of Christ. The Church has always taught that those who may not drink from the Chalice still receive the whole Christ, Body and Blood, soul and divinity. In the same way, those who would drink only of the Chalice, receive the same whole Christ. While it is commendable to receive both the consecrated Bread and the Precious Blood whenever possible so that the signs of eating and drinking Christ's Body and Blood will be more apparent, the whole Christ is present in either species alone.

Holy Communion

The Priest quietly says a short prayer to prepare himself to receive Holy Communion, he genuflects before the Blessed Sacrament, and shows the consecrated elements to the people, saying:

Behold the Lamb of God,
behold him who takes away the sins of the world.
Blessed are those called to the supper of the Lamb.

These words, taken from the Book of Revelation 19:9, echo John the Baptist's cry before the Baptism of Jesus in the Jordan River and look forward to the time when we will sit at the heavenly banquet in the Kingdom of Heaven. In a very real sense, we participate in those moments when we answer the Priest with the words of the good Centurion:

Lord, I am not worthy
that you should enter under my roof,
but only say the word and my soul shall be healed.

Like the Centurion who went to Jesus asking that his servant be healed (Mt 8:5-13), we know that we are not worthy for Jesus to enter into our lives. But, like the Centurion, we trust in God's mercy, knowing that the power of Christ's mercy to free us from our sins is greater than even our weaknesses. Once the Centurion had professed his faith in Jesus' power to heal, the Lord responded to him: "You may go; as you have believed, let it be done for you." Having repented of our sins, we now approach the table of the children of God to receive the bread of life and the cup of eternal salvation.

The Priest then quietly prays a brief prayer to prepare to receive Holy Communion. Once he has received, he distributes Holy Communion to the faithful.

How We Receive Holy Communion

The reception of Holy Communion is one of the most intimate moments in the life of every Catholic. The great mystic and Doctor of the Church, Saint Thérèse of Lisieux, writes eloquently of the first time she ever received Holy Communion:

> I knew that I was loved and said, "I love You, and I give myself to You forever." Jesus asked for nothing, He claimed no sacrifice. Long before that, He and little Thérèse had seen and understood one another well, but on that day it was more than a meeting—it was a complete fusion. We were no longer two, for Thérèse had disappeared like a drop of water lost in the mighty ocean. Jesus alone remained—the Master and the King.

While every reception of Holy Communion cannot be expected to meet the spiritual and emotional heights of Saint Thérèse, her experience reinforces the importance of preparing our hearts to receive Christ in the Most Blessed Sacrament. We do this just before receiving Holy Communion by praying fervently on the most holy mystery we are about to receive. But even before we come to church, we confess our sins and receive absolution in the Sacrament of Penance, especially if we are aware of any serious sins. For at least an hour, we fast from eating anything at all.

In one of the earliest teachings we possess, dating from just decades after the Lord Jesus had risen from the dead, we read about the importance of being well prepared to celebrate the Mass:

> On the Lord's own day, assemble in common to break bread and offer thanks; but first confess your sins, so that your sacrifice may be pure. However, no one quarreling with his brother may join your meeting until they are reconciled; your sacrifice must not be defiled. For here we have the saying of the Lord: "In every place and time offer me a pure sacrifice; for I am a mighty King, says the Lord; and my name spreads terror among the nations [Mal 1:11,14]."[24]

When we go to receive Holy Communion, we never go alone. The Communion Procession is one of the three great processions of the Mass. The first is the Entrance Procession, where we come to recognize that we are a royal priesthood gathered by Christ our High Priest. The second is the Presentation of the Gifts, where we join our lives to the Sacrifice about to be offered by the Priest. Now, singing a Eucharistic hymn, we come forward as Christ's own people to be fed by him with his own Body and Blood.

As you approach the minister to receive the consecrated bread, bow your head as a sign of veneration of the consecrated bread. The minister will hold the consecrated host before you and say, "The Body of Christ," to which you respond, "Amen."

From the first days of the Church, Christians have spoken this "Amen" with conviction and faith. It is, in the first place, an affirmation of Christ's presence in the Blessed Sacrament, whereby, in the words of Saint Ambrose, "you acknowledge in your heart that you are receiving the Body of Christ."[25]

But it is also an acceptance of the consequences of eating his Body and drinking his Blood, as Saint Augustine reminds the fourth-century residents of Hippo:

> If you are the body and members of Christ, then what is laid on the Lord's table is the sacrament *(mysterium)* of what you yourselves are, and it is the sacrament of what you are that you receive. It is to what you yourselves are that you answer *Amen*, and this answer is your affidavit. Be a member of Christ's body, so that your *Amen* may be authentic.[26]

You may receive the consecrated host either on the tongue or in the hand, at your discretion. For many centuries Christians have received Holy Communion on the tongue as a sign of reverence for this awesome mystery. In the earliest days of the Church, and in our own time, Christians typically received the consecrated host in their hands and then reverently eat it. Saint Cyril taught the newly baptized of fourth-century Jerusalem how to receive Holy Communion in the hand in a passage still used by the Church today:

> When you approach, do not extend your hands with palm upward and fingers apart, but make your left hand a throne for your right hand, the latter is to receive the King; then, while answering "Amen," receive the body of Christ in the hollow of your hand. Next . . . take it in your mouth, being watchful that nothing of it is lost. If you were to lose part of it, it would be like losing one of your own members. If someone were to give you some flakes of gold, would you not guard them very carefully and see to it that you did not lose any and suffer a loss? Should you not therefore watch far more carefully over an object more valuable than gold or precious stones, lest you lose a crumb of it? Then, after receiving the body of Christ, approach his blood. . . .[27]

Once you have received Holy Communion under the form of bread, you may then approach the minister with the chalice. Here too you bow your head as a sign of reverence for the Precious Blood of Christ. Then, after the minister says, "The Blood of Christ," you respond by saying, "Amen" and drink from the chalice.

Sometimes the Body and Blood of Christ are given by a method called intinction, whereby the Priest dips the host into the Precious Blood and, after you say, Amen, places it on your tongue.

Take and Eat, Take and Drink

As they receive Holy Communion, a Communion chant or song is sung, by which the faithful praise God in one voice as they process together to receive their Eucharistic Lord. The Communion song is a processional song, ideally sung by all who approach the altar to receive Holy Communion. After receiving Holy Communion all pray quietly or sing a psalm or hymn together.

PRAYER[28]

I believe, O Lord, but may I believe more firmly;
I hope, but may I hope more securely;
I love, but may I love more ardently;
I sorrow, but may I sorrow more deeply.

I adore you as my first beginning;
I long for you as my last end;
I praise you as my constant benefactor; I invoke you
   as my gracious protector.

By your wisdom direct me,
by your righteousness restrain me,
by your indulgence console me,
by your power protect me.

I offer you, Lord, my thoughts to be directed to you,
my words, to be about you,

my deeds, to respect your will,
my trials, to be endured for you.

I will whatever you will,
I will it because you will it,
I will it in the way you will it,
I will it for as long as you will it.

Lord, enlighten my understanding, I pray:
arouse my will, cleanse my heart, sanctify my soul.
May I weep for past sins, repel future temptations,
correct evil inclinations, nurture appropriate virtues.

Give me, good God, love for you, hatred for myself,
zeal for my neighbor, contempt for the world.

May I strive to obey superiors,
to help those dependent on me,
to have care for my friends,
forgiveness for my enemies.

May I conquer sensuality by austerity,
avarice by generosity,
anger by gentleness,
lukewarmness by fervor.

Render me prudent in planning, steadfast in dangers,
patient in adversity, humble in prosperity.

Make me, O Lord, attentive at prayer,
moderate at meals,
diligent in work, steadfast in intent.

May I be careful to maintain interior innocence,
outward modesty,
exemplary behavior, a regular life.

May I be always watchful in subduing nature,
in nourishing grace,
in observing your law, in winning salvation.

May I learn from you how precarious are earthly
things,
how great divine things, how fleeting is time,
how lasting things eternal.

Grant that I may prepare for death, fear judgment,
flee hell, gain paradise.
Through Christ our Lord. Amen.

FOR DISCUSSION

1. Why is the Presentation of the Gifts such an important rite?

2. In the Introductory Dialogue to the Eucharistic Prayer, what does the Priest mean when he says, "Lift up your hearts"?

3. Discuss the epiclesis and the consecration and why they are both so important.

4. Discuss the Eucharistic dimensions of "our daily bread" and "deliver us from evil."

5. Discuss the Breaking of the Bread and the unity of the Church.

6. Discuss the story of the Centurion and our response to the "Behold, the Lamb of God!"

7. Describe the typical way of receiving Holy Communion.

"... let us give thanks,
offering to God a worship
that is pleasing to Him."

—*Hebrews 12:28*

Chapter 6

Understanding the Concluding Rites

THE entire Mass concludes with the Prayer after Communion, the blessing and dismissal.

Prayer After Communion

The Communion Rite is concluded with the Prayer after Communion, in which we give thanks for the great gifts we have received in this Mass. As with all the other prayers, the people make it their own by the acclamation Amen.

Blessing and Dismissal

To conclude the Liturgy, the Priest blesses the people and the Deacon typically makes use of a spare Roman juridical formula: *Ite Missa Est* (literally, it is over, go!) now translated:

Go forth, the Mass is ended.

Yet the significance of the dismissal is far greater for this sending (*missa*) is spoken to a people transformed by the Holy and Living Sacrifice which they have celebrated and nourished by the Body and Blood of their Savior.

Following the 2008 Synod on the Eucharist, Pope Benedict XVI, at the request of the Synod Fathers, added three new dismissal formulas to the conclusion of the Mass:

Go and announce the Gospel of the Lord.

or:

Go in peace, glorifying the Lord by your life.

or:

Go in peace.

Pope John Paul II, in his final Encyclical, *Ecclesia de Eucharistia*, reflects on the meaning of this dismissal and the implications of the Mass for Catholics as they leave the church building and return to the world:

> Certainly the Christian vision leads to the expectation of "new heavens" and "a new earth" (Rev 21:1), but this increases, rather than lessens, *our sense of responsibility for the world today.* I wish to reaffirm this forcefully at the beginning of the new millennium, so that Christians will feel more obliged than ever not to neglect their duties as citizens in this world. Theirs is the task of contributing with the light of the Gospel to the building of a more human world, a world fully in harmony with God's plan. Many problems darken the horizon of our time. We need but think of the urgent need to work for peace, to base relationships between peoples on solid premises of justice and solidarity, and to defend human life from conception to its natural end. And what should we say of the thousand inconsistencies of a "globalized" world where the weakest, the most powerless and the poorest appear to have so little hope! It is in this

world that Christian hope must shine forth! For this reason too, the Lord wished to remain with us in the Eucharist, making his presence in meal and sacrifice the promise of a humanity renewed by his love. . . . Proclaiming the death of the Lord "until he comes" (1 Cor 11:26) entails that all who take part in the Eucharist be committed to changing their lives and making them in a certain way completely "Eucharistic." It is this fruit of a transfigured existence and a commitment to transforming the world in accordance with the Gospel which splendidly illustrates the eschatological tension inherent in the celebration of the Eucharist and in the Christian life as a whole: "Come, Lord Jesus!" (Rev 22:20).[1]

The Priest and the Deacon then kiss the altar, and with the ministers bow in veneration. They then leave the church in the same way in which they entered. Often a "closing hymn" is sung as the ministers process from the church.

PRAYER[2]

Thanksgiving after Mass

It is traditional for Catholics to remain to give thanks to God after the Mass is finished. Do you remember the story of the ten lepers whom Jesus healed? Only one returned to give thanks. Many beautiful prayers have been used by saints throughout the ages to give thanks to God for the gift of the Holy Eucharist.

I give you thanks,
Lord, holy Father, almighty and eternal God,
who have been pleased to nourish me,
a sinner and your unworthy servant,
with the precious Body and Blood
of your Son, our Lord Jesus Christ;
this through no merits of mine,
but due solely to the graciousness of your mercy.

And I pray that this Holy Communion
may not be for me an offense to be punished,
but a saving plea for forgiveness.
May it be for me the armor of faith,
and the shield of good will.
May it cancel my faults,
destroy concupiscence and carnal passion,
increase charity and patience, humility and obedience
and all the virtues,
may it be a firm defense against the snares of all my
    enemies,
both visible and invisible,
the complete calming of my impulses,
both of the flesh and of the spirit,
a firm adherence to you, the one true God,
and the joyful completion of my life's course.

And I beseech you to lead me, a sinner,
to that banquet beyond telling,
where, with your Son and the Holy Spirit
you are the true light of your Saints,
fullness of satisfied desire, eternal gladness,

consummate delight and perfect happiness.
Through Christ our Lord.
Amen.

FOR DISCUSSION

1. What does it mean to receive a blessing?

2. Talk about the dismissal at Mass and our responsibility to the poor of this world.

3. How, practically speaking, can we give thanks after Mass?

Understanding Those Who Celebrate the Mass

Chapter 7

The People and Participation

WHEN the Constitution on the Sacred Liturgy, *Sacrosanctum Concilium*, was promulgated on December 4, 1963, many thought that its call for "full, conscious, and active participation" on the part of the faithful was something quite new. For, immediately prior to the Council, the experience of most lay people at Mass was one of passivity, as though they were what the Council called "outsiders or onlookers."[1] Liturgy was considered to be the responsibility of the ordained clergy who were alone set aside for sacred functions.

But this idea of full, conscious, and active participation in the Sacred Liturgy did not originate with the Fathers of the Second Vatican Council. It started at the Last Supper with the words "Do this in memory of me" (Lk 22:19).

It continued throughout the ages in every town, time, and place: In darkened rooms where potential martyrs prayed for strength and across long aisles peopled with papal processions, beneath towering gothic spires and in quiet rural chapels; and even, in these centuries, in the parishes and cathedrals of the United States of America.

We often forget just how important to the notion of liturgical participation were the words of Pope Pius X, more than one hundred years ago, who called for the full, conscious, and active participation of all those present in the song of the Church, we also forget Pope Pius XII's stirring call in *Mediator Dei*:

> So that the faithful take a more active part in divine worship, . . . it is very necessary that they attend the sacred ceremonies not as if they were outsiders or mute onlookers, but let them fully appreciate the beauty of the liturgy and take part in the sacred ceremonies, alternating their voices with the priest and the choir, according to the prescribed norms. If, please God, this is done, it will not happen that the congregation hardly ever or only in a low murmur answer the prayers in Latin or in the vernacular.

"A congregation," Pope Pius XII wrote, "that is devoutly present at the sacrifice, in which our Savior together with His children redeemed with His sacred blood sings the nuptial hymn of His immense love, cannot keep silent, for 'song befits the lover.' "

Here is the solid foundation upon which the Fathers of the Second Vatican Council built the liturgical reform that we have experienced in our lifetimes. This participation is both a duty and a right of every individual by consequence of Baptism. It is in Baptism we are made members of the People of God, a chosen race, a royal priesthood, a holy nation, a redeemed people. This text of St. Peter (1 Pet 2:9) is read to the newly baptized on Easter Saturday and is further developed in the ecclesiology of *Lumen Gentium*, nos. 9-17.

Active participation in the Liturgy is then, something far more important than the distribution of functions and roles, but is a fundamental disposition that flows into a whole way of life; those who take an active part in the Liturgy are transformed by it and go out from the liturgical assembly conscious of who they are and who they are called to be.

The Sacrifice of the Heart

Working from the Church's ancient understanding of Baptism, whereby those who are baptized into Christ are thereby called to his table[2] as his children, entitled to eat and drink with the family of the Lord, the Fathers insisted that the purpose of baptized life is participation in the Sacrifice of Christ himself.[3] Echoing Augustine, the Council thereby teaches that [it is your own sacrifice]. In effect, all who are baptized are made priests, able to offer themselves "as a living sacrifice that is holy and acceptable to God" (Rom 12:1). Both in Judaism and in the ancient world, in general, self-offering as a "living sacrifice" was unheard of. Like Christ, however, each Christian baptized into his Death and Resurrection is called to make of his life a living sacrifice of praise.

Such a grasp of the priesthood of the faithful—and hence of the sacrifice of the faithful, as it were—had been lost to the liturgical understanding of many before the Second Vatican Council. With the publication of *Sacrosanctum Concilium* in 1963, it was restored to the Church, and with it, a way of understanding the all-important phrase "full, conscious, and active participation." [4]

Participation Is First of All Interior

Two further essential ideas that illuminate the notion of "active participation" urged by the Council are given in *Sacrosanctum Concilium.* The first is that such participation is never successful unless it is prepared for "with the dispositions of a suitable heart and mind. What [worshipers] think and feel must be at one with what they say; they must do their part in the working of grace that comes from above if they are not to have received it in vain." [5]

This is one boat, I fear, that the Church has too often missed. For while we have spent much time arranging furniture and books and telling people where to stand and what to do, we have not spent enough time or energy moving souls and hearts and people to be more like Christ, so that they might be joined with him in the great sacrifice of praise that is the Liturgy.

Expressing and Fostering Faith

"A common posture, to be observed by all participants, is a sign of the unity of the members of the Christian community gathered for the sacred Liturgy: it both expresses and fosters the intention and spiritual attitude of the participants." [6]

External liturgical action, then, grows from an internal intention. Common liturgical action strengthens that internal or spiritual attitude and is motivated by our common conviction that we are not gathered as strangers or individuals, but as a priestly people, called and made one with Christ on his great sacrifice of praise. Such common external action in turn strengthens our internal, foundational unity in Christ, who is the source of all unity and praise.

The same may be said of the new *Roman Missal's* more extended theological description of who the Priest is at Mass. Perhaps more strongly than any other post-conciliar description of the Priest, the new *Roman Missal* speaks of the primacy of the internal and its determinative role on external participation in the liturgical action:

> When he celebrates the Eucharist, therefore, he must serve God and the people with dignity and humility, and by his bearing and by the way he says the divine words he must convey to the faithful the living presence of Christ.[7]

Here we find an exquisite description of what it means to minister in *persona Christi*. Not just by what he says, not just by where he moves and what he does should the Priest seek to show forth Christ to the gathered liturgical assembly. No. The new *Missal* proclaims that by the way he speaks and by the way he moves the Priest must convey, in dignity and humility, a living sense of the presence of Christ in the Liturgy.

Such participation is informed, internal, and profound. It demands that the person who distributes the Holy Eucharist does so with a full appreciation of not only how to present the Body of Christ for the nourishment of his holy people, but with a deep consciousness of who this priestly people is and with a clear focus on the overwhelming mystery of how Christ, present in the consecrated host, is held before the eyes of each communicant.

It means that lectors who proclaim at the conclusion of each reading that what we have heard is "The word of the Lord," truly believe that God has used their tongues to speak his words to a people whom he has loved unto death.

It means that each person is profoundly focused not on the external bow, response, or gesture the Liturgy demands of them, but on the ways in which that liturgical action joins them to the Church and to their neighbor and, indeed, to Christ in his Paschal Sacrifice.

> This full and active sharing on the part of the people is of paramount concern in the process of renewing the liturgy and helping it to grow, because such sharing is the first, and necessary, source from which believers can imbibe the true Christian spirit.[8]

Conformed to Christ

Each of those present at this holy and living Sacrifice is to be changed into the image of Christ upon the Cross. By our participation in this mystery we fulfill the words spoken to the Priest at his ordination: We know what we are doing, we imitate the sacrifice we celebrate, and we conform our lives to the mystery of the Lord's Cross.

Not that we haven't tried our best to thwart God's plan to make us one: he gives us the peace of Eden and we eat the apple. He gives us brotherly love, and we kill our brother Abel; he gives us a single voice and we give him Babel; he gives us the unity of freedom and we grumble in the desert; he gives us his only Son that we might be one, and we nail him to a tree. God gathers and we disperse. God heals and we shatter. In a never-ending struggle, God looks upon our brokenness and continues to call us to be one in him.

In the beginning God made human nature one and decreed that all his children, scattered as they were, would finally be gathered together as one.[9]

Thus, the first and most essential level of our participation in the Liturgy and in the Church is our participation in Christ's Paschal Death and rising on so intimate a level, that we become the mysteries we celebrate; we are transformed into the image of him whose Body and Blood we eat and drink.

A full participation in such a mystery means a full donation of self. A conscious participation in such a mystery means a conscious dying to my own will and a rebirth to God's will for me. An active participation in such mysteries means that I actively let go of everything I have and embrace only the obedient and active love of Christ who now lives in me.

This is a great wonder that we proclaim and believe. It's a wonder that Pope Paul VI understood in 1966 when he proclaimed:

> The Council has taken the fundamental position that the faithful have to understand what the priest is saying and to share in the liturgy; to be not just

passive spectators at Mass but souls alive; to the people of God responsive to him and forming a community gathered as one around the celebrant.

Look at the altar, placed now for dialogue with the assembly . . . The repository has been opened up, as the people's own spoken language now becomes part of their prayer. Lips that had once been still, sealed as it were, now at last begin to move, as the whole assembly can speak its part in the dialogue with the priest . . . No longer do we have the sad phenomenon of people being conversant and vocal about every human subject yet silent and apathetic in the house of God,. How sublime it is to hear during Mass the communal recitation of the Our Father!

Be then, fervent at the Sunday Mass; hold on to it jealously; endeavor to fill every corner of your parish church, to be part of a host of people surrounding the altar. Say to your priests: make us understand; open the book to us. And learn to sing. A Mass celebrated with the song of the people makes for the full raising up of the spirit. Saint Ambrose—one of the first bishops to introduce sacred singing into the Christian community—expressed this striking thought; when I hear an entire assembly sing *Holy, Holy, Holy Lord God* my spirit is flooded with happiness; nothing in the world can possess such grandeur and majesty.[10]

God has begun this great work in us! Imagine, he chose us! In the sacrifice of Christ Jesus his Son, may he bring it to a good conclusion.

PRAYER[11]

I ADORE You, O Jesus, true God and true Man, here present in the Holy Eucharist, as I humbly kneel before You and unite myself in spirit with all the faithful on earth and all the Saints in heaven.

In heartfelt gratitude for so great a blessing, I love You, my Jesus, with my whole soul, for You are infinitely perfect and all worthy of my love. Give me the grace never more in any way to offend You. Grant that I may be renewed by Your Eucharistic presence here on earth and be found worthy to arrive with Mary at the enjoyment of Your eternal and blessed presence in heaven.

FOR DISCUSSION

1. What particular statement concerning participation at Mass has given you a better understanding of your role as a lay person?

2. Explain how the terms (a) full participation; (b) conscious participation; (c) active participation apply to you.

3. How does the new *Roman Missal* broaden the description of who the Priest is at Mass?

Chapter 8

The Priest at Mass

I CAN'T figure out what I'm supposed to do until I know who I am. Thus priestly identity is the necessary starting point for a search for priestly spirituality.

Who is the Priest supposed to be? There's certainly no shortage of advice available for the Priest seeking an answer to that question.

Some would have him be the leader of an orchestra whose success is measured by the harmony of his parish. Others want their Priest to be the politician whose job it is to convince, cajole, and energize the base. Many want him to have all the qualities of a talk show host, engaging them and making the audience think and respond. Not far away are those expecting him to be an entertainer whose jokes and easy manner keep them coming back week after week. There are even those who want him to be the magician whose mysteries never cease to amaze.

But who does Christ want the Priest to be? The Liturgy helps us to figure that out in two articles from the *General Instruction of the Roman Missal*. The first describes who the Priest is at Mass:

> At Mass or the Lord's Supper, the people of God are called together into unity, with a priest presiding and acting in the person of Christ, to celebrate the memorial of the Lord or Eucharistic sacrifice . . . .[1]

That seems like a fairly standard definition, but let's take a closer look. First, the people do not gather of their own volition, this assembly does not belong to them. They are "called together into unity" by Christ. Like the Priest, they are chosen and assembled into a holy people, a royal priesthood, Christ's own Mystical Body. This is an important starting point because none of us, Priest or people, are ultimately in control. It was not us who chose him, but he who chose each one of us (cf. Jn 15:16).

The Priest has two jobs: to preside over the assembly Christ has gathered and to act in the person of Christ. *In persona Christi* had a hard time of it in the sixties and seventies. Perhaps it was because the culture was increasingly egalitarian, perhaps it was because the Pastor translated *in persona Christi* as "I'm God Almighty." In any case, Priests ordained right after the Council usually cringe when you start to talk about *in persona Christi*, until they understand what it really means.

And that's where our next paragraph from the *General Instruction* comes in:

A priest also, who possesses within the Church the power of Holy Orders to offer sacrifice in the person of Christ, *stands* for this reason at the head of the faithful people gathered together here and now, *presides* over their prayer, *proclaims* the message of salvation to them, *associates* the people with himself in the offering of sacrifice through Christ in the Holy Spirit to God the Father, gives his brothers and sisters the Bread of eternal life, and *partakes* of it with them.

Notice the words used to describe who the Priest is at Mass. They are the same words used to describe the Paschal Sacrifice of Christ upon the Cross;

- The Priest stands at the head of the people (*praeest*) just as Christ our High Priest reigns from the wood of the cross (*regnavit a ligno Deus*) [2] and as "the head of the human race" [3] offers the paschal sacrifice, drawing all things to himself (cf. Jn12:32).

- The Priest presides over their prayer (*praesidet*) just as Christ, who presided over the offering of his own Body and Blood upon the Cross, now "presides invisibly over this Eucharistic celebration." [4]

- The Priest proclaims the message of salvation (*proclamat*) just as he who is the truth and who "enlightens every man" (Jn 1:9), proclaims the Mystery of Faith from the altar of the Cross.

- The Priest joins the people to himself (*sociat*) in offering "his sacrifice and theirs" just as "Christ always truly associates the Church with himself in this great work wherein God is perfectly glorified and the recipients made holy." [5]

- The Priest gives them Christ's body (*dat*) just as Christ first said to his Apostles, "take this, all of you and eat it . . ." and from his pierced heart poured forth "the sacraments destined to impart the treasures of redemption on the souls of men." [6]

- The Priest partakes of Christ's Body and Blood (*participat*) which Christ offered from the wood of the Cross for the salvation of the world. [7]

This is why Pope Pius XII, and the Council Fathers after him, remind us that the actions of the Priest are the actions of Christ, the same Lord who now "offers through the ministry of priests, who then offered himself on the cross; only the manner of offering is different." [8]

What the Priest is called to do, therefore, is to conform his actions to Christ's Paschal Sacrifice. Who the Priest is called to be at Mass is the mirror into which people might look to see, not him, but the Christ who lives in him (cf. Gal 2:20).

In his great encyclical *Mediator Dei*, Pope Pius XII offered a profound reflection on this fundamental truth:

The priest is the same, Jesus Christ, whose sacred Person His minister represents. Now the minister, by reason of the sacerdotal consecration that he has received, is made like to the High Priest and possesses the power of performing actions in virtue of Christ's very person. Wherefore in his priestly activity he in a certain manner lends his tongue, and gives his hand "to Christ." [9]

The work of the Priest, then, is to become like Christ. But if the first part of paragraph 93 of the *General Instruction* provides the Priest's Job Description, the concluding sentence is his performance review:

When he celebrates the Eucharist, therefore, he must serve God and the people with **dignity** and **humility**, and by his bearing and by the way he says the divine words he must convey to the faithful the living presence of Christ.

The Fathers of the Second Vatican Council described the priesthood in these words:

Even though Priests do not possess the fullness of High priesthood. . . . they are nonetheless linked to the Bishop in priestly dignity by virtue of the sacrament of Holy Orders, in the image of Christ the Eternal high Priest. . . . [10]

What is this "dignity of the priesthood"? It is a rank with certain attendant responsibilities.

"Human dignity" imposes the duty to honor the gift of life received as a holy work and to use it for the good for which God intended it, for the Priest, the work of shepherding, reaching, and sanctifying in the person of Christ the High Priest.

As Pope Benedict XVI reminded the seminarians of Rome in 2008, "holiness is the secret of the true success of your priestly ministry."

The "dignity of the priesthood" is not, therefore, a call to triumphalism, but a title of service, in the model of Christ, the High Priest who came to serve and not to be served and who offered his own body upon the Altar of the Cross.

This is why the words *dignity* and *humility* go so well together. The dignity of the priesthood is a kenotic dignity, authentic to the extent that it pours itself out and dies for the other. True presbyteral dignity requires the radical humility of him who died for the very ones who nailed him to the Cross. Unless the Priest becomes the least for the sake of the littlest, he is not living out the priestly dignity he received on the day of his ordination.

We have all known Priests who have understood how priestly dignity is born of humility. Some of them are reading these poor words right now. They are the ones who day by day let go of ambition and pride and seem to thrive on sacrificing, consoling, forgiving, and loving like Christ the High Priest.

As a young boy, I remember an old Priest who I later found out never balanced a checkbook in his life. He was an administrative disaster who could drive any parish into chaos in a matter of weeks. But the people venerated him, not for what he did, but for who he was. He was, as Saint Clare used to say of Saint Francis: *the man of God.*

You knew by the way he moved that you were loved and cared for. When he walked into a room, everyone felt better just for his being there. And when you spotted him at the end of the procession at Mass, you knew there was a God.

So, too, in the way he spoke. There was an inner peace and a calmness that told you everything was now going to be all right. And when he prayed, even in a language I did not yet understand, there was such an easy familiarity between him and his God that you felt you were listening in on two old friends, or the easy conversation of a couple who has been married for fifty years.

So, by his bearing and by the way he spoke the sacred words, this Priest reminded even the children of the presence of Christ.

But where did he get all this from? What book did he read? What workshop did he attend? What vitamins did he take?

The simple truth, of course, is that he prayed. For only by that daily intimacy with Christ in the quiet of his room, in the business of his day, and in the crosses he was called to bear, could he have been conformed to Christ the High Priest. He loved the Lord and spent the whole day with him. Thus, he came to look like him.

PRAYER[11]

My intention is to celebrate Mass
and to consecrate the Body and Blood of our Lord
Jesus Christ
according to the Rite of Holy Roman Church,
to the praise of almighty God
and all the Church triumphant,
for my good
and that of all the Church militant,
for all who have commended themselves to my
prayers
in general and in particular,
and for the welfare of Holy Roman Church.
Amen.

FOR DISCUSSION

1. How do the actions of the Priest at Mass as described in the GIRM and *Mediator Dei* correspond to the actions of Jesus Christ the High Priest?

2. Explain how dignity and humility are the cornerstones of the priesthood.

3. How can God's priestly people and his ordained ministers influence each other's personal sanctification?

Chapter 9

The Deacon at Mass

The Deacon and the Liturgy

Like its predecessors, the newest edition of the *Roman Missal* echoes the Council Fathers who saw normative Eucharistic celebration as Mass celebrated in the local church by the Bishop "surrounded by his presbyterate, deacons, and lay ministers... in which the holy people of God take full and active part, for herein is the preeminent expression of the Church." [1]

From the Council Fathers to the latest edition of the *Roman Missal*, then, the Deacon assumes an indispensable, normative role in the celebration of the Eucharist. Two significant changes in the new *Roman Missal* reinforce this point.

Strikingly, the structure of the *General Instruction* has been altered to describe just two basic forms of Mass: Mass without a Deacon and Mass with a Deacon. Thus, while describing with greater precision the specific roles assumed by the Deacon, the new *Missal* emphasizes the all-pervasive effect that presence has to enhance and alter the shape of the celebration.

Secondly, in an entirely new section, we are told that "after the priest, the deacon, has first place among those who minister in the celebration of the Eucharist." [2]

Two points should be made here. First, this concentration on the importance of the role of the Deacon is nothing new. It echoes the words of Pope Paul VI, who in 1972 observed that: "Since the apostolic age itself the diaconate has had a distinctive and superior rank among these ministries and has always been held in great honor by the Church."[3] In this regard he recalls how Saint Paul explicitly greeted not only the Bishops but also the Deacons (cf. Phil 1:1), and describes in detail the qualifications for this important ministry (cf. 1 Tim 3:8-13).

Likewise, he recalls the great martyr, St. Ignatius of Antioch who described the ministry of the Deacon as the same as "the ministry of Jesus Christ, who was with the Father before all ages and has been manifested in the final time." As Saint Ignatius equates the Deacon's ministry with Christ's, he also recalls the Lord's command to his disciples to love others as he had first loved them.

The Deacon is called to be first of all the minister, after the model of Christ, who came to serve and not to be served. The same Christ who told us that he who would be first should put himself last, should become like a little child and should be the servant of all, is the same Christ who through his Church calls the Deacon first of all the minister. The same Christ who died upon a Cross as they cursed and spat upon him, is the one who calls the Deacon to love others as he has loved him.

Thus, right from the start the definition of *diakonia* as kenotic self-giving and service at both the table of sacrifice and the table of charity must guide us in our reading of the identity and function of the Deacon as envisioned by the latest revision of the *Roman Missal*.

The Role of the Deacon

Paragraph 94 of the new *General Instruction* gives us the reasons for its high estimation of diaconal ministry. The predominance of the Deacon is due both to the high honor in which this order has always been held and to the functions of the Deacon at Mass.

It is precisely those functions which I suggest give us an even clearer picture of who the Deacon is in the eyes of the Church, *lex orandi, lex credendi.* For as the Deacon serves the Liturgy, so he is called to serve the Church and the place he takes in the former is descriptive of the place which belongs to him in the latter.

While I am not suggesting that valid observations about the ministry and identity of the Deacon cannot be derived from other sources, the Liturgy is the privileged place for reflection on the meaning and ministry of the diaconate. In the homily at each Deacon's ordination the Bishop reminds him that among his most basic roles is to "prepare the sacrifice, and give the Lord's Body and Blood to the community of believers." [4] Likewise, the antiphon which accompanies the investiture of the newly ordained Deacon with the stole and dalmatic is accompanied by the singing of Psalm 84 with the antiphon, "Blessed are they who dwell in your house, O Lord."

And those Deacons who dwell in God's house are called to five roles that reveal the essential characteristics of diaconal ministry. Those five roles described by the new *Roman Missal* are Deacon as Servant, Proclaimer, Voice, Invitatory, and Dispenser.

Servant of Bishop, Priest, and Altar

As we have implied above, the Deacon's first role is one of *diakonia.* That role takes on concrete form at Mass as the Deacon is called to assist the Priest or Bishop, but especially at the altar in the Preparation of the Gifts and during the Communion Rite.

St. Polycarp of Smyrna is the first to tell that the Deacon is called upon to be "disciplined in all things, merciful, diligent, walking according to the truth of the Lord, who became the servant of all." Likewise, the *Didascalia Apostolorum*, recalls the words of Christ, "Whoever wants to be great among you must be your servant" (Mt 20:26-27).

All of this is echoed in each Ordination of a Deacon, which is replete with reminders of the *diakonia* to which Deacons are called. In his homily the Bishop reminds us that the Deacon "will help the bishop and his body of priests as ministers of the Word, of the altar, and of charity. They will make themselves servants to all." Shortly thereafter, the Bishop turns to the man who will soon be ordained a Deacon and says: "My son, . . . the Lord has set an example for you to follow. As a deacon you will serve Jesus Christ, who was known among his disciples as the one who served others." Finally, we might recall how the first exchange of the diaconal kiss of peace is accompanied by an antiphon quoting the very words of the Savior: "If anyone serves me, says the Lord, my Father in heaven will honor him."

An intimate and reciprocal connection between the Deacon as minister of charity and servant of the Priest and the altar has been with the Church through the ages, as we are reminded by the following early twelfth century description of the Deacon that mirrors almost to the letter the roles assigned by the new *Roman Missal*:

> It pertains to deacons to assist priests and to minister in all things which are done in the sacraments of Christ; that is, in baptism, in chrism, in the paten and chalice, to carry the oblations and place them on the altar, to take care of and decorate the table of the Lord; to carry the cross, and to read the . . . gospel to the people. . . . To deacons also pertain the recitation of prayer and the reading of names of new catechumens. The deacon admonishes all to hear the Lord; he gives peace and he announces . . . deacons receive the texts of the gospel that they may know themselves to be preachers of the gospel of Christ.[5]

How, then, does the new *Roman Missal* call upon the Deacon to serve the altar and the Priest?

- In the preparation of the liturgy, the Deacon should see to it that the necessary vessels and vestments are properly arranged for the celebration. He should also see that the liturgical books are properly prepared, and that the texts for the celebration are marked with ribbons.
- The Deacon accompanies the Priest at almost all times and may offer the introductions and directions in place of the Priest. He assists with incense and the sprinkling with Holy Water and

is seated near the chair so that he might be available to direct any and all practicalities. If catechumens are present, the Deacon may dismiss them before the Profession of Faith.

- Most importantly, the Deacon prepares the altar and assists the Priest in receiving the assembly's gifts or may receive them himself. He prepares the chalice and hands the gifts to the priest, who places them upon the altar.

- The Deacon assists with the breaking of the bread. As an ordinary minister of Holy Communion, the Deacon also assists with the purification of sacred vessels.

- During the Eucharistic Prayer the Deacon assists with the care and even elevation of the chalice and the incensation of the consecrated elements. The new *Roman Missal* prescribes that while for most of the Eucharistic Prayer the Deacon stands near the altar when his ministry involves the chalice and Missal, "as a rule" he kneels from the epiclesis to the elevation of the chalice.[6] "As much as possible, the Deacon stands back from the altar, slightly behind the concelebrants." [7] Three principles seem to dictate the posture of the Deacon during the Eucharistic Prayer: First, that he be well positioned to perform his role as principal assistant to the Priest; second, that it be clear that the Deacon is performing diaconal assistance and not concelebrating and third, that the Deacon model the posture of the faithful.

Thus the rites of the Church make clear that *diakonia* means service and expresses the inextricable link between the diaconal ministry of charity and the liturgical *diakonia*. For just as the Eucharistic celebration is the source of all authentic Christian spirit and the summit of the entire Christian life, what the Church does at Liturgy is the prototype for what she does in life. The Deacon servant of the poor is thus the Deacon servant of the altar.

Proclaimer of the Gospel

The second role of the Deacon in the new *Roman Missal* is that of Proclaimer of the Gospel.

From the tenth century, the presentation of the *Book of the Gospels* at the ordination of a Deacon has signified that the Deacon was a minister of the liturgical proclamation of the Gospel. The Ordination Rite recognizes the diaconal ministry of the word in the rite of presentation:

Receive the Gospel of Christ, whose herald you are.
Believe what you read,
teach what you believe,
and practice what you teach.

When he carries the *Book of the Gospels* in the entrance procession, the book is "slightly elevated." [8] When arriving at the altar with the *Book of the Gospels*, he does not bow, but immediately places the *Book of the Gospels* on the altar and then kisses the altar at the same time the priest does.[9] Greater detail is given to the

Deacon's role in the proclamation of the Gospel as well. He is to bow when asking for the blessing and when taking the *Book of the Gospels* from the altar.[10] A description of the optional kissing of the *Book of the Gospels* by the Bishop is likewise included. The Deacon may proclaim the readings, but only in the absence of a qualified reader.[11] Likewise, the homily may, on occasion, be given by the Deacon.[12]

Voice of the Needy

The third role envisioned by the new *Roman Missal* is the Deacon as the Voice of the Needy.

From the earliest days of the Church, the intention of the Apostles in establishing the diaconate as first expressed in Acts is made clear. As one early Church document relates, it is the role of the Deacon to be the "one who shows love for orphans, for the devout and for the widowed, one who is fervent in spirit, one who shows love for what is good."[13]

This is why the Deacon is the ordinary minister of the Kyrie, all litanies, and even the general intercessions. He articulates the "cry of the poor" because he is the minister most intimately acquainted with the pains, sorrows, and struggles of those most in need of our prayers. He is, in a very real sense, their voice, both in the Liturgy and in the world. For, in a sense, the general intercessions are the prototype of diaconal prayer.

Invitatory to Prayer

The fourth role of the Deacon is to be the issuer of invitations, the invitatory of a rite made flesh.

The Deacon assumes this role not because he is removed from the people, but precisely because he is a man chosen from among men to serve the needs of all. It is his intimacy with the assembly that empowers him to be the one who directs common posture and gesture and exhorts the members of the liturgical assembly to pray. Thus does he call upon the people to exchange the Sign of Peace, direct them when they are to kneel, to bow their heads, or perform some ritual gestures, as at the solemn blessing or prayer over the people at the end of Mass, or in the solemn intercessory prayers of the Good Friday Liturgy.

Bearer of the Cup of Salvation

From the earliest days of the Church, the Deacon has been the minister of the Precious Blood. He bears the cup of eternal salvation and ministers it to God's holy people. Thus the new *Roman Missal* prescribes that at Communion, the Priest himself gives Communion to the Deacon under both kinds. When Communion is given to the faithful under both kinds, the Deacon ministers the chalice. After Communion has been distributed, the Deacon, at the altar, reverently consumes any of the Blood of Christ that remains.[14]

All this begins with the sixth promise taken by the Deacon at his ordination: to shape his way of life "always according to the example of Christ, whose body and blood [they] will give to the people." This promise, in turn, is rooted in the earliest prayer for the ordination of a Deacon found in the *Apostolic Tradition* of Hippolytus, which mentions but one specific task assigned to the Deacon: "to bring forward [in your holy of holies] the gifts which are offered to you by your appointed high priests." [15]

Diakonia in the Model of Christ Jesus

We began this brief reflection by recalling Saint Ignatius' description of the Deacon as a minister in the model of Christ Jesus. I wish to conclude by calling all Deacons to see everything they do at Mass as an opportunity to make themselves vessels through which Christ Jesus can be made present to his holy people. Yet just as Christ's perfect sacrifice was accomplished through his kenotic self-emptying, so Deacons are called to empty themselves each time they seek to serve the Sacrifice of the altar.

When the Deacon comes to serve, he must empty himself from all selfish concerns. He must see himself as servant of the Liturgy and never its master. He must minister to the priest and to the altar with the humility of him whose very Body and Blood were offered on the altar of the Cross.

When he comes to proclaim the Gospel, the Deacon must empty himself of all his worldly wisdom that he might be filled only with the wisdom of God. He must decrease so that the Word of God might take root in him and those who hear his voice may hear not him, but Christ Jesus who lives in him. His acclamation of "the Gospel of the Lord" must ring authentic and true.

When he proclaims intercessions or invites the people

to prayer, the faithful must recognize in the Deacon the trustworthy and compassionate man to whom they may go with any of their needs. The poor must know him as their friend. Orphans must see him as their father, and all who are alone, afraid or confused must see in him a refuge in the model of Christ Jesus. All must have such trust in his prudence and charity that his wise guidance is spontaneously welcomed.

Finally, all who receive the Savior's Precious Blood from the Deacon's hands must receive the chalice as from one who knows the meaning of sacrifice, of being poured out for God's people, and of striving for holiness of life. The Deacon, too, must take up the cup of salvation as one whose very life is a hymn of praise to the Lord. For the cup he bears is his salvation and a model of the life to which he is called as a Deacon.

What the new *Roman Missal* and the Church ask of the Deacon is to become more like Christ. To participate in his Paschal Death and Resurrection by how he lives and how he prays, by what he does and who he has become.

This is the mystery of diaconal ministry at the altar. It is the mystery of the Church and the mystery of all who are called to the Supper of the Lamb!

PRAYER[16]

Lord, make me an instrument of Your peace.
Where there is hatred, let me sow love.
Where there is injury, let me sow pardon.

Where there is friction, let me sow union.
Where there is error, let me sow truth.
Where there is doubt, let me sow faith.
Where there is despair, let me sow hope.
Where there is darkness, let me sow light.
Where there is sadness, let me sow joy.

O Divine Master, grant that I may not so much seek to
be consoled as to console,
to be understood as to understand,
to be loved as to love.
For it is in giving that we receive.
It is in pardoning that we are pardoned.
It is in dying that we are born to eternal life.

St. Francis of Assisi

FOR DISCUSSION

1. Describe the Deacon's primary role of *diakonia.*

2. How is the Deacon a "voice for the needy" at Mass
and in the world?

Afterword

Translation of the Mass

SOME of the words we use to speak to God at Mass are soon about to change. After nearly 40 years of using the same translations of these ancient Roman liturgical texts, you and I are about to experience something really quite remarkable.

In the next several pages I'd like to suggest how these new translations can help you and me and the whole Church to deepen our appreciation of the immemorial rites and prayers of the *Roman Missal*. It is a journey that takes us back almost 2000 years, to the place where the prayers of our *Missal* began, in Sacred Scripture, in prayers from the lips of the Fathers of the Church, in the same prayers that nourished the faith of St. Francis and St. Clare, of St. Dominic and St. Scholastica, and all the saints of all the ages.

Did you know that almost all the Opening Prayers, the Collects that we use at Mass have their origin over 1000 years ago? And the Church has sought to preserve this great heritage of faith because she believes that the way she prays defines who she professes to be. Indeed, as both the *General Instruction* and *Liturgiam Authenticam* tell us, the Roman Catholic Church is best defined by her liturgical books.

We have worked hard for all these centuries to preserve the sacred Latin texts, and what a great opportunity we now have to translate and proclaim them with an authenticity and fidelity that give new birth to their beauty, their power, and their meaning.

That's what Pope John Paul II meant when he approved the fifth post-conciliar instruction on the implementation of the Sacred Liturgy under the title *Liturgiam Authenticam.* While praising "the great work of renewal of the liturgical books of the Roman rite" that has been accomplished in the post-conciliar reform, the Holy Father noted the need in our own day for the improvement or correction of liturgical translations formulated under theories now known to be incapable of conveying the true power of the Latin liturgical texts.

> In order that such a rich patrimony may be preserved and passed on through the centuries, it is to be kept in mind from the beginning that the translation of the liturgical texts of the Roman Liturgy is not so much a work of creative innovation as it is of rendering the original texts faithfully and accurately into the vernacular language

So what kind of translations are these to be? Are they to be so slavishly literal that they read more like a mathematical expression in human speech? Will they employ words and phrases so alien to our experience that no one will have any idea what they're talking about? I'm sure you've heard the rumors and read the reports of the new liturgical translation: that they're a rejection, some would say, of the original vision of the Council Fathers to promote full, conscious, and active participation even in the manner of the translation of liturgical texts.

But this is just not so. For when Pope Paul VI first described liturgical translation as a search for "the voice of the Church" in our day and our language, he was articulating a vision of vernacular translations that would authentically convey the original Latin liturgical prayer in beautiful and understandable English.

Which is exactly what the instruction *Liturgiam Authenticam* calls for:

> So that the content of the original texts may be evident and comprehensible even to the faithful who lack any special intellectual formation, the translations should be characterized by a kind of language which is easily understandable, yet which at the same time preserves these texts' dignity, beauty, and doctrinal precision.

Now that's quite a tall order! Authentic, doctrinally precise, and beautiful. That's why it's taken the Bishops of the English-speaking world nearly fifteen years to consider and approve a new translation of the *Roman Missal*.

Just a word about the process. In order for a liturgical translation to be confirmed by the Holy See, it must first be approved by more than two-thirds of the Bishops of an Episcopal conference. That's why ICEL serves as a mixed commission of the 11 major English-speaking countries: ICEL is a factory of sorts for the production of English-language liturgical texts. Each of the translations that are included here has gone through more than a dozen drafts over the past 15 years. Each of the Bishops of the English-speaking world has been consulted innumerable times on the principles of translation, the quality of each individual text, and finally on the words we should use when celebrating the Mass.

The *Vox Clara Committee*, consisting of prominent Bishops and scholars from throughout the English-speaking world, advises the Holy See on the final editing of these texts.

So what are you to expect from these new translations? Yes, indeed, they are more accurate, doctrinally precise, and more reflective of the beauty of the original Latin, but what will that mean?

Let's start with some examples from the Order of Mass, one segment of the *Roman Missal* that has been approved by the Bishops and confirmed in the Holy See. Let's start with the *Confiteor*:

Two simple changes make this prayer more faithful to its Latin original. In line 3, *nimis* was never translated. Now we say: *greatly* sinned. And the old familiar triplex *mea culpa* (through my fault) has been restored. Not a very big change, but a far more accurate translation.

That's not very different than another of the people's parts: the *suscipiat*. Again, we find a phrase missing from our present translation. The Latin asks the people to pray that *meum ac vestram sacrificium* (my sacrifice and yours) be acceptable to God. This phrase has been restored in order to help us appreciate that all the sacrifices of the faithful gathered together join to the one perfect sacrifice of Christ.

And then there's the *Ecce Agnus Dei*. What does the Latin text really say?

> Behold the Lamb of God, behold him who takes away the sins of the world. Blessed are they who have been called to the supper of the Lamb.

Notice that this is one of the most profoundly eschatological texts in the whole Roman Liturgy. The Fathers of the Church used to say that at this moment a little window opened between heaven and earth and all time and all space disappeared. Blessed are they who have been called to the supper of the Lamb and the great heavenly nuptial banquet! For at this moment we are one with that heavenly banquet and with every person who in every place has ever come to eat and drink from God's holy altar.

And we respond with the words of the centurion:

> Lord, I am not worthy that you should come under my roof, but only say the word, and my soul shall be healed.

Such changes in translation are simple and select what the Latin text has truly said for the past thousand years.

And then there's the Gloria. Pray the text on page 51 out loud if you will. Poets, musicians, theologians, and pastors have worked with translators for many years to give us this text. And just how much did they change?

Was it 25% of the text, 35% of the text, or 55% of the text of the current English Gloria changed in this new translation? What do you think?

In fact, more than half of the lines of this hymn have been changed in the new translation. Are you surprised? That's the sign of a good translation. A quick look at the 1970 translation shows us why so much had to be changed. *Et in terra pax hominibus bonae voluntatis*, becomes "peace to his people on earth."

The acclamations *Laudamus te, benedicimus te, adoramus te, glorificamus te.* . . . are moved down two lines, and one of the lines is never translated. Indeed, as you can see, the entire hymn is re-imagined and restructured, following a theory which was not so much translation as recomposition.

But the new translation, the work of musicians, poets, and translators working together, is both accurate and suitable for sung prayer.

Perhaps the most common dialogue in the Liturgy of the Roman Rite consists of the greeting

Dominus vobiscum
et cum spiritu tuo

Presently translated as:

The Lord be with you.
And also with you.

This is one of a very few translations specifically corrected by the instruction *Liturgiam Authenticam*. We will now respond: And with your spirit. Why? For two reasons:

First, because "And also with you" is clearly a mistranslation, as every other major language, except for Dutch, attests: In Italian it's (*E con il tuo spirito*), in French (*Et avec votre esprit*), in Spanish (*Y con tu espíritu*) and in German (*Und mit deinem Geiste*). In each instance, the Latin word *spiritu* is translated precisely.

Et cum spiritu tuo is used only in response to the Priest, and exceptionally for the Deacon, from the earliest days of the Church. It is from the Fathers that we learn its meaning. For each time the Priest is about to embark on an important liturgical action, he turns to the people and says: "The Lord be with you. May the Lord who has gathered you together, prepare you for the important work we are about to do."

And they respond, "And with your spirit." "May you, our Priest, may the charismatic gifts you received in your Ordination now be with you that you might be prepared for this important work."

For in Ordination the Bishop prayed over each one of us: " . . . in the desert you implanted the spirit of Moses in the hearts of seventy wise men; and with their help he ruled your people with greater ease."

As it was then, so it is today.

Will the changing of this frequently used dialogue be easy? Certainly not! But it is absolutely necessary for accuracy and to maintain the very reason why the response was introduced into the Roman Liturgy almost two thousand years ago.

The new translations of the *Roman Missal* involve a new way of speaking for the Priest at Mass. For the first time we will be exposed to the voice, ever ancient and ever new, of Roman Catholic Liturgical Prayer.

It is not a voice that is colloquial or informal. While it is often striking in its directness and simplicity, the rhetoric of the *Roman Missal* is rich with meaning. Each time we return to the beauty of these poetic texts our minds will be challenged and our hearts will be moved in yet a different way. The texts are thick, memorable, and deeply theological.

They are not unlike great rhetoric that we have known in our country. Like the second inaugural address of Abraham Lincoln at the close of the Civil War:

> With malice toward none, with charity for all, with firmness in the right as God gives us to see the right, let us strive on to finish the work we are in, to bind up the nation's wounds, to care for him who shall have borne the battle and for his widow and his orphan, to do all which may achieve and cherish a just and lasting peace among ourselves and with all nations.

Or President Reagan on the day that the space shuttle Challenger was destroyed in a tragic accident:

> The crew of the space shuttle Challenger honored us by the manner in which they lived their lives. We will never forget them, nor the last time we saw them, this morning, as they prepared for their journey and waved goodbye and "slipped the surly bonds of earth" to "touch the face of God."

Each of these pieces of great American rhetoric is formal, yet profoundly intimate, in the same manner that the Collects, Prefaces, and other prayers of the *Roman Missal* convey both the transcendence and the immanence of God's incarnate love.

We find such richness in the new translation of the Roman Canon, the first Eucharistic Prayer. The extended introductory dialogue leads us into the prayer:

℣. The Lord be with you.
℟. And with your spirit.
℣. Lift up your hearts.
℟. We lift them up to the Lord.
℣. Let us give thanks to the Lord our God.
℟. It is right and just.

It is right and just! You can almost see some ancient Roman magistrate setting his seal upon a document: it is right and just! Just as God's holy people gathered together for the celebration of the Mass, having been invited by the Priest to lift up their hearts and give thanks to God, we respond: it is right and just.

Then come the extraordinary opening words of the first Eucharistic prayer. The lesson is unique, used only in the blessing of baptismal water and the Church's most solemn hymn: the Te Deum. *Te igitur Clementissime Pater*, the Priest begins. What a curious way to begin a prayer! *Te!* To you! But that's just the point. From its very opening words the Roman Canon reminds us that this great prayer is addressed to God our heavenly Father. How do we begin the prayer in our present translation?

We come to you Father. . . . But how does the new translation render *Te igitur Clementissime Pater*?

To you, therefore, most merciful Father,
we make humble prayer and petition. . . .

And then there are the Collects and the Prefaces, whose ancient richness is so evident in the new translations that they will become a rich source for our homiletic, catechetical, and theological reflection for decades to come.

Listen to the Collect for the annual commemoration of the dedication of a Church:

O God, who year by year renew for us the day
when this your holy temple was consecrated,
hear the prayers of your people
and grant that in this place
for you there may always be pure worship
and for us, fullness of redemption.

A similar richness is found in the Commons of the Blessed Virgin Mary, but here we find a surprise as well. Fully realized for the first time that each time we commemorate she who was conceived without sin we become conscious of our own sinfulness and our need for her intercession:

Grant us, O merciful God,
protection in our weakness,
that we, who keep the Memorial of the holy Mother of
     God,

may, with the help of her intercession,
rise up from our iniquities.

Another example:

Pardon the faults of your servants, we pray, O Lord,
that we, who cannot please you by our own deeds,
may be saved through the intercession
of the Mother of your Son and our Lord.

What a wonderful phrase: "we who cannot please you by our own deeds."

The third Collect from the Commons reflects the same theme but within the context of a typical Christmas meditation on the coming of Christ our Light:

O God, who willed that your Word,
begotten from eternity,
should come forth from the womb
of the Blessed Virgin Mary,
grant, we pray, through her intercession,
that he may light up our darkness
with the splendor of his presence,
and from his fullness give us joy and peace.

The richness of these prayers is drawing from their thick formality and poetic character, yet at the same time these rhetorical forms make them uniquely capable of expressing intimacy.

The difference between translations that truly reveal the original character of Roman liturgical prayer and the former translations is particularly evident in the Collects for the three Masses of Christmas.

Here's a new translation of the Mass for the Christmas Vigil:

O God, who gladden us year by year
as we wait in hope for our redemption,
grant that, just as we joyfully welcome
your Only Begotten Son as our Redeemer,
we may also merit to face him confidently
when he comes again as our Judge.

Notice how it weaves together all the themes of the Advent season: expectation for the Lord who is coming, hope, joy, and judgment.

But notice how flat and didactic, stripped of all poetic enthusiasm, our present translation reads. Additionally it fails to convey the indispensable role of God's grace:

God our Father,
every year *we rejoice*
as we look forward to this feast of our salvation.
May we welcome Christ as our redeemer,
and meet him with confidence when he comes to be
our judge.

The light imagery in the next Christmas Collect makes us think of the churches flickering lights and the smell of candle wax at midnight Mass:

O God, who have made this most sacred night
radiant with the splendor of the true light,
grant, we pray, that we, who have known the mysteries of his light on earth,
may also delight in his gladness in heaven.

And finally, listen to the Collect for Christmas Day, which from the earliest days of the Church has been prayed when men and women like you and me respond to God's call to celebrate the wonders of his Incarnation. It begins with our creation, recalls our need to be restored, and concludes with words used at the comingling of water and wine at every Mass:

> O God, who wonderfully created the dignity of human
>   nature
> and still more wonderfully restored it,
> grant, we pray,
> that we may share in the divinity of Christ,
> who humbled himself to share in our humanity.

These new translations provide us with a challenge. We will need to study them, to pray them, and to make them part of ourselves. But if we do, the immemorial voice of the Church will once again proclaim the wonders that God has done for us in every generation.

We have a challenge before us, but we also have a wonderful opportunity. For the first time in the post-conciliar liturgical reform we will be exposed to the prayers of the Roman rite in their fullness, in their beauty, and in their deep theological meaning.

Glossary of Terms

Act of Penitence: Rite in praise of God's mercy celebrated after the greeting in most Masses.

Agnus Dei: Chant asking Christ, the Lamb of God, for mercy, sung during the fraction rite.

Alleluia: An acclamation of Paschal joy, sung outside of Lent during the Gospel procession.

Altar: Table of sacrifice, usually of stone, on which the Mass is offered.

Ambo: Large lectern from which the sacred scriptures are proclaimed.

Amen: Ancient acclamation signifying assent and used in liturgical and devotional prayers.

Anamnesis: "Remembering" of Christ's Paschal death and rising in the Eucharistic Prayer.

Apostles' Creed: Oldest of the Professions of Faith, based on baptismal promises.

Baptism: First of the sacraments, which washes away original sin and grafts the believer on to Christ and his Church.

Basilica: Roman church form consisting of a rectangular hall, columns, and an apse.

Blessed Mother: A title of Mary, the Mother of Jesus.

Blessed Trinity: Three Persons in one God: Father, Son, and Holy Spirit.

Blessed Virgin: Another title of Mary, the Mother of Jesus.

Book of the Gospels: Ornate and honored liturgical book containing the four Gospels.

Breaking of the Bread: Oldest name for the Mass, also the rite of breaking the consecrated bread into smaller pieces for the faithful.

Cathedra: Chair reserved for the Bishop in his cathedral church.

Chalice: Ornate cup, usually of metal, used to hold the Precious Blood.

Collect: Opening Prayer at the Mass.

Communion, Reception of: Rite for the distribution of the Body and Blood of Christ to the faithful.

Confiteor: First of the Acts of penitence, a medieval prayer confessing sins and asking for God's mercy.

Consecration: Central moment of the Eucharistic Prayer at which the words of Christ are spoken over the bread and wine that they might become consecrated into his Body and Blood.

Council of Trent: Sixteenth-century Council, called in response to the Reformation, at which major liturgical reforms were instituted.

Deacon: Third of the ranks of "Holy Orders," an order of service to the Eucharist and those in need.

Didache: Compilation of prayers and commentaries dating possibly as early as first-century Syria.

Ekklesia: Greek word for Church, rooted in the word for "calling together."

Emperor Constantine: Fourth-century Roman Emperor who legalized Christianity.

Epiclesis: Part of the Eucharistic Prayer, asking the Father to send the Holy Spirit upon the gifts of bread and wine and the gathered assembly.

Eternal Word: Title of Christ, the word through whom all things were made (cf. Jn 1:1ff.).

Eucharist: Name for the Mass and for Holy Communion, comes from the Greek work for "thanksgiving."

Eucharistic Prayer: Central prayer of the Mass in which bread and wine are consecrated as the Body and Blood of Christ.

Final Doxology: Hymn of praise to God which completes the Eucharistic Prayer; all respond "Amen."

Fraction: Another name for the Breaking of the Bread at which the bread is broken for distribution to the liturgical assembly.

Genuflection: A gesture of reverence made by bending the knee with origins in royal court ritual.

Gloria: Ancient hymn to the glory of God sung at more solemn celebrations, also known as the "angelic Hymn."

Good Friday: Two days before Easter, when Christians commemorate the Crucifixion.

Gospel Procession: Procession with the *Book of the Gospels* accompanied by candles and incense, to commemorate the coming of Christ in the Holy Gospel.

Gospels: Four books of the New Testament containing the words and actions of Jesus Christ.

Gothic: Type of late medieval architecture using light and soaring arches to convey the transcendence of God.

Holy Communion: The consecrated bread and wine, the Body and Blood of Christ.

Holy Water: Blessed water, used to remind us of our Baptism.

Homily: Sermon preached by an ordained minister at Mass.

Incense: Aromatic resins burned on charcoals to honor sacred objects or persons and to remind us of our prayers rising up to God.

Intercessions: Prayers or intentions offered to God.

Intinction: Distribution of Holy Communion by dipping the consecrated host into the Precious Blood.

Kyrie: Ancient Greek acclamation asking the Lord for mercy, used in the Act of Penitence.

Lamb of God: Title of Christ, the Paschal Lamb who is sacrificed for our sins.

Lay Ministries: Lectors, acolytes, and others who, though not ordained, perform a liturgical function by virtue of their Baptism.

Lector: Lay minister who proclaims the non-Gospel readings at the Liturgy.

Liturgy: Public prayer of the Church celebrated in accord with immemorial rites.

Liturgy of the Eucharist: Second half of the Mass, centering around the Sacrifice of Christ and the reception of Holy Communion.

Liturgy of the Word: First half of the Mass, centering on the proclamation of the Word of God.

Lord's Prayer: The "Our Father," taught to the disciples by the Lord himself.

Martyr: A Christian who has been killed because of his faith.

Mystery of Faith: Proclamation of the Paschal Mystery after the consecration at Mass.

Nicene Creed: Typical form of the Profession of Faith, first composed at the fourth-century Council of Nicaea.

Offertory Chant: Song sung during the Presentation of the Gifts by the people at Mass.

Paschal Sacrifice: Christ's Death on the Cross and rising from the dead on the third day.

People of God: Title of those who have been baptized into Christ, also the Mystical Body.

Posture: Bodily attitude at Mass, preferably taken in common to express unity of the faithful.

Prayer of the Faithful: Prayers for the needs of the Church and the world at Mass, also called the Universal Prayer.

Prayer over the Gifts: Final Prayer of the Preparation of the Gifts at Mass.

Precious Blood: Another name for the Blood of Christ.

Preface: First part of the Eucharistic Prayer, praising God for his great works.

Preparation of the Gifts: Part of the Mass devoted to preparing the gifts of bread and wine.

Priest: Second Order of the of Sacrament of Holy Orders, acts in the person of Christ at Mass and consecrates the gifts of bread and wine.

Priest's chair: Chair in the church reserved for the Priest as chief teacher and shepherd.

Procession with the Gifts: Presentation of the bread and wine by a representative group of the faithful at Mass.

Profession of Faith: Credal statement proclaimed together at Mass, summarizing Catholic beliefs.

Responsorial Psalm: Psalm and antiphon sung in response to the First Reading at Mass.

Rite of Peace: Ancient Mass rite recalling Christ's gift of peace and exchanging a sign of it.

Roman Canon: First of the Eucharistic Prayers at Mass, also called Eucharistic Prayer I.

Roman Missal: Book containing the Mass prayers and rites.

Sacrosanctum Concilium: Constitution on the Liturgy promulgated as the first document of the Second Vatican Council in 1963.

Saint Ambrose: Bishop of Milan (338-397 A.D.), a famous preacher counted among the "Church Fathers."

Saint Augustine: Bishop of Hippo in Northern Africa (354-430 A.D.), a famous preacher counted among the "Church Fathers."

Saint Ignatius of Antioch: The third Bishop of Antioch, martyred in the arena at Rome (35-107).

Saint Jerome: A monk, scholar, and one of the first translators of the Bible (347-420 A.D.), counted among the "Church Fathers."

Saint Justin: A Christian apologist who suffered martyrdom in Rome (100-165 A.D.) and whose writings counted among first testimonies to how the Mass was celebrated.

Sanctus: The "Holy, holy" chant sung after the Preface of the Eucharistic Prayer.

Savior: Title given to Jesus Christ, who by his death and rising saved us from sin and death.

Scriptures: The books of the Bible.

Second Vatican Council: Council called by Pope John XXIII and meeting from 1962 to 1965, commissioned a major reform of the Sacred Liturgy.

Sign of the Cross: Ancient gesture of prayer recalling the Blessed Trinity and the Cross of Jesus Christ.

Suscipiat: Prayer offered by the people for the Priest during the Preparation of the Gifts.

Tabernacle: Box or safe where the consecrated bread (Body of Christ) is stored after Mass.

Thurible: Metal bowl suspended by chains in which incense is burned on hot charcoals.

Vernacular: Individual modern language into which the liturgy is often translated from its Latin original.

Notes

Introduction: What Is the Mass?

[1] RS, no. 2; cf. 1 Cor 5:7.

[2] Cf. SC, no. 41, GIRM, no. 16.

Chapter 1: Where the Mass Came From

[1] Saint Justin, *Apologia* I 65 and 67, 3-5, from L. Deiss, *Springtime of the Liturgy. Liturgical Texts of the First Four Centuries*, translated by M. J. O'Connell (Collegeville: The Liturgical Press, 1979), 92-94.

[2] *Didache* 9-10, from L. Deiss, *Springtime of the Liturgy. Liturgical Texts of the First Four Centuries*, translated by M. J. O'Connell (Collegeville: The Liturgical Press, 1979), 74-76.

[3] Council of Trent, Decree *De observandis et evitandis in celebratione missarum.*

[4] SC, no. 21.

[5] SC, no. 51.

[6] SC, no. 14.

[7] Pope Paul VI, Apostolic Constitution *Missale Romanum*, 1969.

Chapter 2: What We Do at Mass

[1] SC, no. 7; cf. GIRM, no. 20.

[2] "who was concieved by the Holy Spirit, born of the Virgin Mary."

[3] STL, no. 2.

[4] USCCB (2007), *Sing to the Lord*, no. 13.

[5] Pope Benedict XVI, Angelus, December 18, 2005.

[6] Cardinal Francis Arinze, "Translation and the Liturgy," an Address to the Gateway Liturgical Conference in Saint Louis, Missouri (November 11, 2006).

[7] Cf. GIRM, no. 82.

[8] Cf. GIRM, no. 78.

[9] GIRM, nos. 95-97.

[10] Archbishop Jerome Hanus, OSB, Address to the 1999 National Meeting of Diocesan Liturgical Commissions, in the *BCL Newsletter,* September-October, 1999.

[11] From the *Roman Missal,* excerpted from the Prayer of Preparation for Mass: Prayer of Saint Thomas Aquinas.

Chapter 3: Understanding the Introductory Rites

[1] St. Jerome, *In die dominica Paschale,* II, 52; cf. JP II, Ap Lett *Dies Domini,* no. 2.

[2] Cf. SC, nos. 5-7.

[3] Cf. "A Demonstration of Low Mass" by Msgr. Martin P. Hellriegal, in *Sanctification of Sunday: National Liturgical Week* (The Liturgical Conference, Conception, Missouri, 1949), page 9.

[4] Cf. BLS, no. 63.

[5] Romano Guardini, *Sacred Signs,* 1927.

[6] In fact, when a Bishop celebrates the Mass, he uses this very greeting: *Peace be with you.*

[7] The Deacon or another minister may introduce the Mass in the place of the Priest.

[8] Lucien Deiss, *The Mass* (Collegeville: Liturgical Press, 1992), page 19.

[9] Lucien Deiss, *The Mass* (Collegeville: Liturgical Press, 1992), page 23.

[10] Reverend Paul Bussard, *The Meaning of the Mass*. (P.J. Kennedy and Sons, 1941). page 52..

[11] This story is reported in "Amen: Notes on its Significance and Use in Biblical and Post-Biblical Times," in *The Jewish Quarterly* (October, 1896), page B.

[12] *Comm. in epist ad gal., proem. ad lib.* II, p. 428.

[13] From the *Roman Missal*, excerpted from the Prayers of Preparation for Mass: The Prayer of Saint Ambrose.

Chapter 4: Understanding the Liturgy of the Word

[1] *Commentarii in Isaiam prophetam, Prologus:* 24, 17 A; CCL, no. 73, 1.

[2] DV, no. 21.

[3] LFM, no. 4.

[4] LFM, no. 5.

[5] Cf. LFM, no. 6.

[6] Cf. BLS, no. 61.

[7] Except at Easter time, when it is taken from the Acts of the Apostles.

[8] Cf. GIRM, no. 29.

[9] SC, no. 45.

[10] JP II *ad limina* to Bishops of NW US.

[11] Cf. LFM, no. 17, BOG, no. 8.

[12] Except during Lent, when we fast from singing the Easter Alleluia in favor of another chant, such as, *Praise to you, Lord Jesus Christ, King of Endless Glory!*

[13] BOG, no. 18; cf.*Cæremoniale Episcoporum,* nos. 74 and 141.

[14] Augustine, *Confessions.* LCL I. 240.

[15] LFM, no. 24, citing fn. 45.

[16] GIRM, no. 67.

[17] GS, no. 1.

[18] IOM, no. 96.

[19] From the *Roman Missal:* Prayer to the Most Holy Redeemer.

Chapter 5: Understanding the Liturgy of the Eucharist

[1] SC, no. 47.

[2] Cf. GIRM, no. 71.

[3] Cf. Second Vatican Ecumenical Council, Constitution on the Sacred Liturgy, *Sacrosanctum Concilium*, no. 47; Sacred Congregation of Rites, Instruction *Eucharisticum mysterium,* On the worship of the Eucharist, 25 May 1967, no. 3a, b: AAS 59 (1967), pp. 540-541.

[4] GIRM, no. 72.

[5] Cf. SC, no. 14.

[6] Paul Claudel,"La Messe lá-bas,"in *The Mass: Christians Around the Altar,* by the community of Saint-Severin (Geoffrey Chapman, London: 1958), page 33.

[7] Cardinal Suhard, quoted in *The Mass, Source of Sanctity,* Francois Charmet, SJ (South Bend, IN: Fides Publishers, Inc., 1964), pages 142-143.

[8] Cf. 1 Cor 16:1; 2 Cor 8:9, and CCC, no. 1351.

[9] St. Justin, *Apol.* I, 67: PG 6, 429.

[10] Cf. GIRM, no. 75.

[11] Wash me, O Lord, from my iniquity, and cleanse me from my sin.

[12] SC, no. 48.

[13] Cf. CCC, no. 1353.

[14] Saint Cyril of Jerusalem, Cat. XXIII, 7: PG 33, 1114ff, quoted in SC, no. 13.

[15] Cf. SC, no. 13.

[16] CCC, no. 1354.

[17] CCC, no. 1354.

[18] Saint Augustine, Serm. clxxii, 2, P.L., XXXVIII, 936.

[19] CCC, no. 1032.

[20] Dionysius of Alexandria, quoted in a Letter to Pope Sixtus II, recorded in Eusebius, *The History of the Church*, VII, 9, translated by G.A. Williamson (Pengiun Books: Baltimore, 1963), page 29, as quoted in *The Church at Prayer, V. II*, by A.G. Martimort, revised by Robert Cabie and translated by Matthew J. O'Connell (Collegeville: The Liturgical Press, 1986), page 106.

[21] Saint Augustine, Sermon 57.

[22] Saint Augustine, Sermon 17.

[23] Rubric, Order of Mass.

[24] The *Didache* (90 AD), 14:1.

[25] Saint Ambrose, *De Sacramentis* IV, 25.

[26] St. Augustine, Serm. 272 (PL 38:1247), as quoted in *The Church at Prayer, V. II*, by A.G. Martimort, revised by Robert Cabie and translated by Matthew J. O'Connell (Collegeville: The Liturgical Press, 1986), page 118.

[27] St. Cyril of Jerusalem, *Mystagogical Catechesis* V: 27, as quoted in *The Church at Prayer, V. II*, by A.G. Martimort, revised by Robert Cabie and translated by Matthew J. O'Connell (Collegeville: The Liturgical Press, 1986), page 120.

[28] From the *Roman Missal:* The Universal Prayer attributed to Pope Clement XI.

Chapter 6: Understanding the Concluding Rites

[1] EE, no. 20.

[2] From the *Roman Missal:* Thanksgiving After Mass: Prayer of Saint Thomas Aquinas.

Chapter 7: The People and Participation

[1] SC, no. 14.

[2] Cf. SC, no. 9.

[3] Cf. SC, no.10.

[4] SC, no. 14.

[5] SC, no. 11.

[6] GIRM, no. 42.

[7] GIRM, no. 93.

[8] SC, no.14.

[9] LG, no. 13.

[10] Paul VI: Homily at the Parish of Mary Immaculate, Rome, March 27, 1966.

[11] Prayer of Adoration and Petition: *Catholic Book of Prayers* (Totowa, NJ: Catholic Book Publishing Corp., 2005), page 79.

Chapter 8: The Priest at Mass

[1] GIRM, no. 27.

[2] *Vexilla Regis*

[3] MD, no. 75.

[4] CCC, no. 1348.

[5] SC, no. 7.

[6] MD, no. 17.

[7] Cf. Council of Trent, Sess. 22, c.1, as cited in *Mediator Dei*, no. 76.

[8] CCC, no. 1367.

[9] MD, no. 69.

[10] LG, no. 28, as cited in the Introduction to the Ordination of a Priest, no. 5.

[11] From the *Roman Missal* from the Prayer of Preparation for Mass: Formula of Intent.

Chapter 9: The Deacon at Mass

[1] SC, no. 112.

[2] GIRM, no. 94.

[3] *Ministeria quaedam.*

[4] Rite of Ordination of a Deacon.

[5] Peter Lombard, *Sentences* (PL 192:903), as translated and quoted in Echlin, *The Deacon in the Church*, pages 84-85 [*Sententiae IV*, dist. xxiv].

[6] GIRM, no.179.

[7] GIRM, no. 215.

[8] GIRM, no. 172.

[9] Cf. GIRM, no. 173.

[10] Cf. GIRM, no. 175.

[11] Cf. GIRM, no. 176.

[12] Cf., GIRM, no. 66.

[13] *Testamentum D.N. Iesu Christi* 1, 38: I. E. Rahmani, ed. and tr. (Mainz, 1899) 93.

[14] Cf. GIRM, no. 182.

[15] Apostolic Tradition of Hippolytus (c. 215). H. Boone Porter, *The Ordination Prayers of the Ancient Western Church* (Alcuin Club Collections, no. XLIX; London, 1967), p. 12, adapted. See also Paul F. Bradshaw, *Ordination Rites of the Ancient Churches of East and West* (New York: Pueblo, 1990).

[16] Prayer for the Grace to Help Others: *Catholic Book of Prayers* (Totowa, NJ: Catholic Book Publishing Corp., 2005), pages 206-207.

St. Joseph *Weekday Missals*

This handy-size, PERPETUAL Weekday Missal contains all the Weekday Masses with their options. The arrangement follows the liturgical year, and Volume I is for Weekdays only from Advent to Pentecost for both Year I and Year II. Volume II covers Pentecost to Advent.

No. 920/09 Vol. I—Advent to Pentecost **19.95**
Brown Vinyl ISBN 978-0-89942-931-1
No. 921/09 Vol. II—Pentecost to Advent **19.95**
Blue Vinyl ISBN 978-0-89942-932-8

No. 920/23 Vol. I—Advent to Pentecost (Zipper) **29.95**
Black Bonded Leather ISBN 978-0-89942-933-5
No. 921/23 Vol. II—Pentecost to Advent (Zipper) **29.95**
Black Bonded Leather ISBN 978-0-89942-934-2

St. Joseph *Sunday Missals*

The one all-inclusive, complete and permanent Sunday Missal. It contains all the official Mass prayers for Sundays and Holydays that are now in use throughout America.

It Includes the complete 3-year cycle of Sunday readings **(for years, A, B & C)**. It includes all the prayers from the Sacramentary... plus all the presidential prayers. These prayers are repeated for each cycle of readings to make this Missal "easy to use" and to eliminate unnecessary page-turning.

Catholics of all ages will truly treasure this excellent Missal destined to last a lifetime. Calendar to year 2016.

No. 820/09—Red flexible vinyl cover **21.00**
ISBN 978-0-89942-820-8

No. 820/23—Burgundy bonded leather-zipper binding...........**32.00**
ISBN 978-0-89942-836-9

Giant Type Edition

A new, easy-to-use Sunday Missal that gives all the Mass texts for the 3-year-cycle. Easy-to-read, easy-to-carry, easy-to-keep. Size $5^{1}/_{4}$ x $7^{1}/_{2}$. Color illustrations.

No. 822/10—Burgundy, flexible cover, burgundy edges
ISBN 978-0-89942-822-2 ....**24.95**

Complete Gift Box 3-Volume Set

Attractive and durable gold embossed black imitation leather case contains the two-volume Weekday Missals (Vols. I & II) and the complete one-volume Sunday Missal (years A, B, C). All three volumes are bound in rich bonded leather featuring our popular new zipper closure. All bindings are sewn for long-lasting durability.

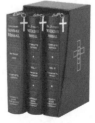

No. 825/23 ISBN 978-0-89942-838-3..**89.00**

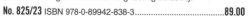